IBERIA
CHRONICLES

FOOTBALL CHRONICLE

IBERIA CHRONICLES

A BRIEF HISTORY OF SPANISH AND PORTUGUESE FOOTBALL

First published by Pitch Publishing, 2020

Pitch Publishing
A2 Yeoman Gate
Yeoman Way
Worthing
Sussex
BN13 3QZ
www.pitchpublishing.co.uk
info@pitchpublishing.co.uk

A CIP catalogue record is available for this book
from the British Library.

ISBN 978 1 78531 726 2

Typesetting and origination by Pitch Publishing
Printed and bound in India by Replika Press Pvt. Ltd.

CONTENTS

AUTHORS:

Alex Goncalves, Billy Munday, Brad Jones, Dan Parry, Daniel Allen, Danny Lewis, Edd Norval, Gareth Thomas, Jake Sandy, Joe Brennan, Josh Butler, Karan Tejwani, Kaustubh Pandey, Kristofer McCormack, Michael Gallwey, Nathan Motz, Rahul Warrier, Ryan Plant, Somnath Sengupta and Will Gittins

WELCOME TO
IBERIA CHRONICLES

IN AUGUST 2018, we started Football Chronicle with the simple idea of producing original long-form football content. For over 18 months, we published pieces from a collection of writers looking to get their words out, helping them pursue their passions in football writing whilst working towards our own ambitions of making a mark in modern journalism.

It was an enjoyable and productive period during which we've made huge strides forward. Early in 2020, we decided to step it up a notch and move to print, which is why we're so pleased to present our first book, *Iberia Chronicles*. Our online stories covered tales from the world over, going into niches like Lebanon and Rwanda or the glory of the Netherlands and Argentina. For our first print edition, we've specifically chosen two countries with a storied history in the game – Spain and Portugal – bringing together a team of 20 writers who have covered the nations in depth over the years.

The next 20 chapters bring you stories of the greats including Luis Aragonés and Bobby Robson, iconic teams such as Boavista and Deportivo La Coruña, tales of cities and stadiums, wins and losses and a whole lot more. Questions are asked and answers are raised: what is Portugal's footballing relationship with Africa? Why are so many Spanish stadiums named so unconventionally? Why couldn't the Basque region continue their dominance for long in Spain? *Iberia Chronicles* is the culmination of several months of research and effort.

We would like to thank the people that have supported this book, a piece of passionate work produced by a group that loves this beautiful game. Without that support, we wouldn't be doing what we have been doing, either online or kicking off this venture in print. We also appreciate the support given to us by Pitch Publishing, specifically Jane Camillin for making this book a reality as well as Duncan Olner for the wonderful cover design. Also, we greatly value the time and love taken by the writers to be a part of this. Projects like this are the work of a collective.

Rahul Warrier and Karan Tejwani

SPAIN

LUIS ARAGONÉS: THE GODFATHER OF SPANISH FOOTBALL

by Billy Munday *(@billymunday08)*

THE 1920 Olympic Games saw Spain come back from Antwerp with two medals. Both of them were silver. One came in polo. The other in football. The Spanish team were labelled '*la Furia Roja*' – the Red Fury – by those that watched them in Belgium that summer for their tenacious, aggressive approach to the game. Rafael Moreno Aranzadi, or 'Pichichi' – peewee – as he was dubbed due to his slender build, netted the final goal of their campaign in a 3-1 victory over the Netherlands in the silver-medal match. That '*Furia Roja*' tag stuck with Spain for the decades to follow, highlighting their ferocious style of play but, other than their Euro 1964 triumph, their style brought them very few successes.

Struggling with identity around the turn of the 21st century, Spain were crying out for a steady hand to steer them down the right path. Their journey to the top started with the final whistle in Lisbon as Nuno Gomes's sole goal for Portugal had sealed their return flight home at the group stages of Euro 2004. Iñaki Sáez stepped back down to his role with the U21s after touching down in Madrid as the Spanish Football Federation searched for a new man to lead this promising yet underperforming crop of players.

The chosen one had just spent the last few months sunning himself in the dugout at Son Moix. Luis Aragonés, in his second spell in charge of Real Mallorca, had plenty of experience and quite the reputation. An Atlético Madrid icon, his footballing career had started on the other side of town. At the age of 20, he left Real Madrid due to a lack of opportunities in the 1960s. Loans at Recreativo de Huelva and Hércules had demonstrated his goalscoring prowess but had not convinced the board of the newly crowned European champions. After a short diversion to Asturias and Real Oviedo in particular, the attacking midfielder ended up down south in Seville.

Real Betis, who'd just had their royal prefix reinstalled after it was originally stripped under Franco's dictatorship, were riding the crest of a wave at the start of the 1960s having earned promotion back to Spain's top flight and stayed there under the watchful eye of president Benito Villamarín. In Aragonés's final season in Heliópolis, *Los Verdiblancos* challenged Real Madrid at the top of LaLiga. With just three fixtures of the league campaign left, Atlético Madrid visited the Estadio Benito Villamarín having struck a deal to sign three pillars of Betis's success: right-back Colo, defensive midfielder Jesus Martinez and Aragonés. In the days between the announcement of their moves and the match, Colo and Aragonés would travel to play for Spain in Ireland for a Euro qualifier.

Aragonés would be the only one of the three Atlético-bound players to feature against their future employers, with Colo and Martinez pulling out injured. With the visitors 1-0 up at half-time, the soon-to-be Atlético talisman scored two and set up another against them in an eventual 4-2 victory for Betis. Despite his impressive form, the 25-year-old was left out of the Spain squad that went on to lift the European Championship trophy as hosts at the Bernabéu. Nevertheless, Aragonés would arrive in the capital that summer anyway as Vicente Calderón welcomed him to the Metropolitano, Atlético's old home in the university district of Madrid. It was there and later on at the Estadio Vicente Calderón where it all took off.

Despite not playing as a central striker, Aragonés was mightily prolific. During his time in charge of the national team, Spain were blessed with some special hitmen, with a couple of new kids coming on to the block. Both Fernando Torres and David Villa have always commended his influence on their careers. The pair, then 22 and 25 respectively, were each given a bundle of trust by their boss at the 2006 World Cup, starting ahead of Real Madrid's Raúl in the opening game in Leipzig. After Xabi Alonso's first against Ukraine, the following three goals were scored between the two, with Villa hitting a double and Torres a single. The relationship between the future Liverpool and Chelsea striker and Aragonés was a particularly tight one, built on parallel personal experiences.

During his playing days at Atlético, Aragonés was held in such high esteem, which only grew with every passing medal he collected. Three LaLiga titles and two Copas del Generalisimo – as the Copa del Rey was called under the dictatorship – to boot for Zapatones – 'big boots'. That nickname didn't come about as a result of any sort of arrogance but the real thwack he could generate from a dead ball. In those three league triumphs, he was in the top two scorers, winning the *Pichichi* alongside Atlético team-mate José Eulogio Gárate and Real Madrid's Amancio in 1970. There was more success on the European stage, too.

Aragonés notched six goals in the opening two rounds of the European Cup in 1970/71, including a hat-trick in the return leg of the second round against Cagliari. Rinus Michels's Ajax were eventually too much for *Los Rojiblancos* in the last four. That particular hurdle was cleared three years later as Atlético progressed past Celtic to reach their first European Cup Final against Bayern Munich in Brussels. With the game goalless in the second half of extra time, Aragonés stepped up and welled in a free kick to open the scoring and almost certainly seal the title. With the clock ticking over to 120 minutes and the red and white ribbons sitting by the cup, Katsche Schwarzenbeck rifled the ball into the bottom corner from distance to set up a replay two days later. Bayern cruised through the replay in the end, meaning this was the first segment of the heartbreaking European Cup Final trilogy for Atlético. You know the other two.

Those big boots were hung up that same summer having kicked their way to the top of Atlético's scoring charts. They still sit there today on 172 goals. Of all the club's top attacking talent since, Antoine Griezmann has come closest to those first few places, but he was still 39 strikes behind Aragonés when he left for Barcelona in 2019. Torres is one of the few to exceed the mythical goal machine in Atlético appearances. His first six came with the club in the Segunda around the turn of the 21st century and, after three different coaches had failed to get them straight back up, Aragonés was installed in the Calderón dugout for the seventh time. His first six spells had yielded plenty of silverware.

There was one LaLiga title, three Copas del Rey, one Supercopa de España and one Intercontinental Cup, but this was a different challenge. Typical of the man, Aragonés passed it with flying colours, guiding Atlético back to where they belonged after a two-year absence. Contrary to Diego Simeone's current regime, Aragonés's Atlético were geared up for goals and a teenage Torres was making the most of it, wasting no time once he'd featured in the top flight for the first time. He made a fool of Frank de Boer in a sensational 3-0 win over Barcelona on his way to becoming the club's top scorer – by quite a distance, too. Six goals separated him and second-place Luis García in the scoring charts. This was all helped by the tutelage of the very best.

'Aragonés was my teacher, the one who kept my feet on the ground and put the brakes on my ambition until I was ready for the next step,' Torres wrote in *El Mundo* when his former boss passed away in 2014. 'He would say to me every day, "Kid, you know nothing about nothing", and I came to realise that he did that because he was preparing me for the future and because he believed in me.' That belief was still there, burning away in the back of the youngster's head, when the pair's paths crossed again with Spain just a couple of years later. Torres had already been given his senior bow by Sáez, but it was under Aragonés that he really flourished.

Luis García benefitted from a familiar face in the international dugout too, hitting a hat-trick in the first leg of Spain's World Cup play-off against Slovakia in 2005 to virtually punch the ticket to Germany for the finals. There, Torres netted three times during the group stages – including that fourth against Ukraine in Leipzig – as Spain progressed with a perfect record. Although Villa had handed the advantage Spain's way during their last-16 tie, Frank Ribéry, Patrick Vieira and Zinedine Zidane ensured that France's flag would by flying in the last eight instead. It was only six months further down the line that crisis talks began to creep up as Aragonés's side went down to a David Healy-inspired Northern Ireland and Sweden in Euro 2008 qualifying. The Spanish Football Federation had reportedly contacted Miguel Ángel Lotina about taking over before Aragonés beat Argentina four days after defeat in Solna. The following week, he penned a new deal to take him through to the Euros having already verbally agreed it after the World Cup.

With control over his own future, 'big boots' started to stamp his authority on Spain. Raúl didn't receive another call-up as Torres and Villa took on the goalscoring responsibilities. Xavi and Andrés Iniesta bonded in the middle as Cesc Fàbregas and David Silva were also introduced to the fold. At the back, Carlos and Carles – Marchena and Puyol, that is – had made the central positions their own while Sergio Ramos and Joan Capdevila emerged as the starting full-backs. Holding it all together was Marcos Senna, who combined poise and power to make the midfield his own. Eight wins out of their final nine qualifiers saw them come into the Euros as major contenders.

Aragonés, who'd seen, lived and breathed Spain's 'Furia Roja' years, didn't abandon that particular style, but blended it with a revolutionary new brand. The essence of tiki-taka is known and it was on those pitches in Austria and Switzerland where the seeds were laid for its future success. Everyone in that Spain team was comfortable on the ball, some more than others.

Their short passing style dictated the metronome of those three weeks to a snappy Spanish tempo. Guus Hiddink's Russia couldn't keep up with the rhythm set in Innsbruck as they danced to Senna, Xavi and Iniesta's beat. Villa's treble and Fàbregas's fourth were followed by two more goals against Sweden on the same stage four days later.

This was a tighter, tougher affair as Zlatan Ibrahimović matched Torres's opener ten minutes before the break, although the Spanish defence left much to be desired. Just as a point apiece seemed the most likely outcome, Spain's striking duo came good again. Villa, this time, found the net just in time. There was another thrilling finale in Salzburg as a much-changed Spain left it late against Greece. Dani Güiza was the hero on this occasion, sealing a quarter-final encounter with the world champions in Vienna. Senna, Xavi, Iniesta and Silva were entrusted with the controls but Italy's defensive system wasn't easy to breach, not even after 120 minutes.

Xavi and Iniesta were discarded on the hour mark, with Fàbregas and Santi Cazorla replacing them. Both of the substitutes, 21 and 23 respectively, held their young nerves in the subsequent shoot-out. Where Daniele de Rossi and Antonio Di Natale failed and Casillas prevailed, they nailed it. The then-current Arsenal man, rather than the future one, slid in the winning spot kick after whispering to the ball on the walk up, urging it to go in. Letting the ball do the work was a simple but effective summary of Spain's sensational style that summer and it served them well in the semi-final against Russia too. But they had to do it without their top scorer.

Aragonés left just one striker on the pitch, Torres, when he took off the injured Villa during the first half. With an extra body in deeper areas in Fàbregas, Spain ran Russia into the ground as they had done two weeks before in their opening match. It took 50 minutes of wearing them down before their performance was rewarded on the scoreboard. After Xavi's first, Güiza and Silva added two more before time was up as a Spanish symphony sounded out across the Austrian capital. There would be one final song at the Ernst-Happel-Stadion that Sunday against a typically efficient Germany team.

Michael Ballack was at the heart of it and, despite Aragonés referring to him as 'Wallace' in his team talks, the Spanish players got the message. One final piece of advice was saved for his adopted son before kick-off: 'He grabbed me on my own in the tunnel, put me against the wall, got hold of me by the chest and said: "This is our moment kid, you are going to go out there and score twice and we are going to be champions of Europe." Then he made the sign of the cross on my forehead and let me go out to play,' Torres recalled to *Marca* later down the line. The Liverpool striker didn't score twice, but once was enough anyway.

The silverware and medals that followed are tangible evidence of Aragonés's influence on the game as his approach reached all four corners of the globe. The less tangible signs of his legacy come between the four corners of the football pitch as Barcelona share the ball around, as coaches like Pep Guardiola ask their teams to keep the ball and as you, like many others, have fallen in love with the Spanish game.

SPAIN'S FOOTBALL STADIUMS: A GATEWAY TO THE PAST

by Daniel Allen *(@danwritesstuff)*

IN RECENT years, the ever-increasing sums of money which circulate throughout football have seen the game take new shape. Although insights into the world of football's super-rich generally take the form of scandalous transfer fees and exorbitant player wages, a preoccupation with sporting finances has escalated off the field also. However, as commercialism permeates through every corner of the sport, and modern football continues to be enveloped by ubiquitous corporate sponsorship, the notion of a pure and romantic game slowly wears away.

Take the world of football stadiums, for instance. Once, grounds across the world stood in honour of local heritage, or people instrumental in the building of great clubs. But now, these very stadiums act as glorified advertising hoardings, giving prominence, instead, to multinational corporations, media conglomerates and global super-banks.

Across Europe, Juventus and Bayern Munich rake in millions playing in grounds named after the financial company Allianz. While in England, Manchester City pushed forward with their problematic partnership with Etihad, and Arsenal are not long off leaving the historic Highbury for a stadium now sponsored by Emirates. Oftentimes, clubs move grounds and it's the sponsorship deals that follow through, frequently altering a stadium's name to a more unfancied one.

This process has happened in Spain, too. The need to compete at the highest financial level recently saw Atlético Madrid move from the iconic Estadio Vicente Calderón, to the multi-million-euro Wanda Metropolitano. The Calderón not only represented all that was genuinely authentic and intimidating about Atléti, but it also played host to some of the national game's most formative matches.

Atlético Madrid and Spain hero Luis Aragonés christened the stadium, scoring its first goal in 1966. Rather poetically, the arena was the fitting home for a tribute to his life almost 50 years later. The ground also hosted three matches at the 1982 World Cup, welcoming Michel Platini's timeless French side. It witnessed the incredible comeback against Johan Cruyff's Barcelona in 1993 too, when *Los Rojiblancos* found themselves three down at half-time only to fight back and win 4-3. And, most recently, it was the fortress upon which Diego Simeone built the club's incredible, duopoly-breaking title success of 2014.

Beyond its use as a definitive footballing amphitheatre, the stadium also spoke to something innate within the makeup of Atlético Madrid. Vicente Calderón was Atléti president between 1964 and 1980, and then again from 1982 to 1987. During his presidency, *Los Rojiblancos* embarked on one of their most successful periods, culminating in a heartbreakingly narrow European Cup Final defeat to Bayern Munich in 1974.

On the pitch, Calderón helped Atléti build a world-class outfit, while off it, the Spaniard was instrumental in the construction of the stadium which they called home for over half a century. Calderón's achievements were such that Atlético renamed the stadium in honour of their president, where the club remained until it moved away in 2019 and opted to cash in on ground-naming rights.

For the most part, however, Spanish clubs have resisted the lure of commercialisation. As such, the nation stands in contrast to the majority of Europe, holding out from sponsored name changes and opting instead to keep a shred of the nostalgic game alive. Interestingly, many of the stadium names across the highest levels of Spanish football take inspiration from local geography.

Oddly, one of the country's oldest stadiums, Valencia's Estadio de Mestalla, shares its name with a nearby irrigation canal. Villarreal, meanwhile, recently decided to change the name of their home, El Madrigal, to Estadio de la Cerámica in commemoration of the local tile industry. Elsewhere, Rayo Vallecano's Campo de Fútbol de Vallecas bears the name of their barrio in Madrid; the working-class neighbourhood has hard-left roots and provides a strong sense of identity to the humble club of the capital.

Others' names, too, hold a symbolic as well as geographical meaning. Athletic Club's Estadio de San Mamés, for instance, is so-called after a Catholic saint. So the story goes, Mammes of Caesarea was a child martyr, thrown to the lions by the Romans. Expecting him to be devoured by the beasts, Mammes instead tamed the animals with the word of God. The importance of religion is not purely mythological for the Basque club, though. San Mamés is also known as The Cathedral, showing how football has a profoundly spiritual appeal, and that their devoted fans' journey to the stadium each week is akin to a sort of pilgrimage.

Perhaps the oddest of all names derived from local heritage, though, is that which graces SD Huesca's stadium. Remarkably, the roots for their ground, Estadio El Alcoraz, go back almost a thousand years to 1096. The name references the Battle of Alcoraz, a siege fought between Peter I of Aragon and Al-Musta'in II of Zaragoza. The fight is believed to have taken place near the grounds of Huesca's stadium, which now ensures that far less bloody battles take place on a bi-weekly basis.

For Real Valladolid further east, inspiration for the naming of their stadium came instead from the world of literature. Estadio José Zorrilla is named after the 19th-century poet and playwright who was a prominent figure in the Spanish romantic movement. Himself a son of Valladolid, Zorrilla's most renowned work is the play *Don Juan Tenorio*. A story of burning romance and moral conflict, the epic displays a not too different kind of passion and melodrama to the one offered up on the Valladolid football field each week.

As José Zorrilla stands testament to, the most common stadium names across the highest levels of Spanish football remain those of people. For the most part, these take the form of men more directly linked to the game as influential presidents and administrators, crucial in the shaping of Spain's most popular sport on both a local and national level, take pride of place.

In Seville, for example, Real Betis's Estadio Benito Villamarín is so-called after one of their most influential presidents. Now seen as a crucial point in the club's history, Villamarín's shrewd financial management rescued the team from their post-war slump and enabled the club to purchase the Estadio Municipal Heliópolis outright. As a show of appreciation, the ground was quickly renamed in his honour.

That is, until 1997, when egocentric Betis owner Manuel Ruiz de Lopera renamed the stadium eponymously. Lopera took over the club in 1992, with Betis staring down the barrel of financial ruin. Incredibly, just six years later, *Los Verdiblancos* broke the world-record transfer fee when they signed the tricky winger Denilson from São Paulo. The Brazilian forward was a major flop, and his signing ultimately encapsulated the sort of erratic mismanagement which had come to define Lopera's reign.

Although the Spaniard was eventually replaced as president, Lopera hung around the club as majority shareholder for many years. But, with Betis's form gradually dropping, and calls that charges of fraud be filed against Lopera intensifying after he was revealed to be siphoning money from the club, the Spaniard was deposed entirely in 2010. Understandably, Betis quickly voted to rename the stadium back in honour of the more deserving Villamarín.

For Betis's cross-city rivals Sevilla, the story of their stadium name is a more tragic one. In their infant years, Sevilla were nomads, roaming from football field to football field in search of a place to call home. In 1928, the club constructed Estadio de Nervión, but it quickly became inadequate in the face of Sevilla's rapidly expanding appeal. As such, club president Ramón Sánchez-Pizjuán quickly tasked himself with finding a more suitable stadium, one more able to match the club's growing ambition.

The project soon stalled, and it was not until 1954 that Manuel Muñoz Monasterio, fresh from designing the impressive Estadio Santiago Bernabéu, was selected as the stadium's architect. Suddenly, Pizjuán's grand vision was coming to life, but mere weeks before construction of the stadium was due to begin, the president fell ill and soon passed away.

The man tasked with replacing Sánchez-Pizjuán was his deputy Ramón de Carranza. The new leader was determined to make Pizjuán's dream a reality and, just weeks after his death, broke ground on Sevilla's new home. Once completed, Carranza officially opened the stadium and declared it would be named in honour of their late president, who was so tragically denied the chance to see the footballing coliseum in all its glory.

Remarkably, in nearby Cádiz, Carranza too has a stadium named after him. A prominent local politician, Carranza gives his name to the ground of southern minnow Cádiz CF. Its presence there, however, has become a major cause of controversy as Carranza was not just a football man, but was also a significant figure during the Spanish Civil War. A vehement Francoist, the would-be Sevilla president was involved in the plot to overthrow the Second Republic in its very earliest stages. Not only was he central to the coup, further investigations into Carranza have revealed him to be a man uncompromising in his pursuit of socialists and trade unionists.

In a rapidly changing Spain, which has recently started to tackle the deep-rooted trauma caused by the infighting of the Civil War, and has finally begun to re-evaluate how it commemorates Franco's dictatorship after passing the Law of Historical Memory, it is surprising to see Carranza's name still hold place at Cádiz CF. As such, questions of whether bestowing such prominence on to a Francoist, and a particularly dogmatic one at that, are still justly being asked.

Elsewhere, perhaps the most famous Spanish stadium named after a person, and one slightly less shrouded in controversy, is Real Madrid's Estadio Santiago Bernabéu. Although Bernabéu's name has become more synonymous with steel, concrete and plastic seats over the years, his impact on *Los Blancos* goes much deeper than merely giving his name to their iconic stadium.

Bernabéu joined the Madrid club as a child around the beginning of the 20th century. Although the team was still amateur, Bernabéu is widely believed to have been a proficient and effective forward, even in the cruder days of the Spanish game. He then retired towards the end of the 1920s before assuming various administrative positions and even briefly taking over as manager.

However, after the breakout of the Civil War put an end to the national game, Bernabéu, a fascist in republican Madrid, was forced to flee the capital. When Franco eventually claimed victory over the ousted Republic in 1939, Bernabéu returned home, but found the club, like the city, in ruins. Real Madrid's slow rebuild could now begin, but it was not truly set in motion until Bernabéu was officially appointed president in 1943.

Not content there, Bernabéu was then an instrumental figure in the formation of a new European Cup. Moving to establish dominance over the continent, the president set about building a world-class side. Adding to a team already packed with some of the finest talents in Spain, Bernabéu snatched the maverick Alfredo Di Stéfano from rivals Barcelona, signed the great Hungarian forward Ferenc Puskás, and finished off a string of world-class acquisitions by bringing in the little French genius Raymond Kopa. In a feat unmatched to this day, Real Madrid won the first five editions of the European Cup, and Bernabéu's vision of domestic and continental hegemony had been truly realised.

Despite briefly donning a pair of football boots himself, Bernabéu is primarily remembered for his achievements in the boardroom. Rather oddly, therefore, that means only one club at the highest level of Spanish football operate in a stadium named after a man chiefly known for playing the game. That team is Getafe, and they call the Coliseum Alfonso Pérez home. As is now to be expected, even their story is not so straightforward.

Alfonso was born and raised in Getafe, but as a child he was snapped up by local giants Real Madrid. It was in the capital that Alfonso made his breakthrough, and after a few seasons floating around the first team, he copped a move to Real Betis. At *Los Verdiblancos*, the striker played the best football of his career and soon earned a call-up to the Spanish national team for Euro 2000.

In that tournament, Pérez scored the goal which would come to define his career. It was the final group match, and Spain were 3-2 down to Yugoslavia and staring in the face of elimination. Four minutes into added time, Gaizka Mendieta's penalty gave Spain the faintest of hope. Then, with barely seconds left to play, the ball was pumped into the Yugoslav box. There, it dropped to the feet of Pérez, who fired the ball into the net and completed an incredible comeback for the delirious Spaniards.

His performances at Euro 2000, plus his consistent exploits for Betis, earned Alfonso a dream move to Barcelona. In truth, his career in Catalonia never really took off, and after just two seasons Alfonso would, in his own words, 'return home'. The 'home' Alfonso was referring to, though, was not his beloved Getafe, but was in fact his adopted club Real Betis. Incredibly, despite his name gracing the stadium of his hometown Getafe, Alfonso Pérez never so much as kicked a ball for his boyhood club.

On the whole, therefore, while the majority of the footballing world looks to cash in on advertising and ground sponsorship, it is refreshing to see Spanish clubs hold out and keep a shred of the nostalgic game alive. Their stadium names, from bizarre local heritage and influential, if controversial, presidents, to nationally renowned writers and hometown hero players, provide us with a rich and storied history. Above all, they remind us that football is not shaped solely by ubiquitous advertising campaigns, but is in fact a game which is continually enhanced by national culture, local history and passionate people.

BASQUE DOMINANCE

by Somnath Sengupta *(@baggiholic)*

IT WAS a gloomy and rain-swept day in April. Just like the weather, the Estadio El Molinón in Gijón also presented a grim spectacle with its muddy turf and stands full of black umbrellas. With a few seconds left on the clock Real Sociedad mustered one last, desperate attack; a cross was punted by Periko Alonso. It was cleared and fell to Alberto Górriz, who swiped at it and his miskick scampered towards Jesus Zamora. There was no time for sophistication as he pulled back his right foot and delivered a hammer blow from close range. When Zamora's shot hit the net, the Real Sociedad players and travelling faithful went berserk.

Real Sociedad has scored prettier goals in its 110-year history but there isn't a more famous one. The picture of Zamora pulling the trigger is arguably the most famous moment in the club's history and can be seen in bars and walls around San Sebastián. It was the last kick of Real Sociedad's 1980/81 LaLiga campaign. With that goal, the *Txuri-urdinak* (blue and whites) captured their first LaLiga title, etching the date of 26 March 1981 forever in the hearts of its fans.

It also sparked off an unprecedented era of domination of the Basque clubs in the Spanish top flight. From 1981 to 1984, each of the four LaLiga titles would end up either in San Sebastián or in Bilbao, where Athletic Club were at the peak of their powers. It was a stark contrast to how the previous decade had panned out for these clubs.

In the 1970s, the Basque Country found itself between the hammer of violent actions by extremist Basque nationalist group *Euskadi Ta Askatasuna* (*ETA*) and the anvil that was merciless reprisals from the Franco regime. On the field, neither Athletic Club nor Real Sociedad had the best of times. Silverware was scarce and they often found themselves languishing in the lower half of the league table.

The most notable event for both Basque clubs in the 1970s was inarguably the Ikurriña derby. On 5 December 1976, a year after Franco's death, rival captains Inaxio Kortabarria of Real Sociedad and José Ángel Iribar of Athletic Club marched on the field together holding Ikurriña, the flag of the Basque Country which was still banned in Spain. It was an emphatic statement of Basque pride and would go a long way in legalisation of the flag. In tandem, the performances improved as Athletic Club earned back-to-back podium finishes and topped it with a UEFA Cup Final appearance in 1977. However, as the tumultuous decade came to a close, it was their derby rivals that had picked up the baton of supremacy.

A solid, if not spectacular full-back, Alberto Ormaetxea Ibarlucea spent most of his playing career at Real Sociedad. After retirement, he was immediately absorbed in *La Real*'s coaching team and worked as an assistant to Rafael Iriondo, Andoni Elizondo and José Antonio Irulegui. He took over the reins as head coach in 1978 and inherited an experienced, battle-hardened unit thanks to seamless integration with Real Sociedad's academy by his predecessors. Ormaetxea improved consistency, minimised mistakes and turned them into a team that was extremely hard to break down. It was a hard-working, well-organised and functional squad, mirroring the people it represented. Needless to say, *Txuri-urdinak* fans were enamoured by their team and turned their home stadium into a fortress.

In Ormaetxea's first season in 1978/79 his team finished a credible fourth and qualified for the UEFA Cup. Using a simple strategy of winning at home and avoiding losses in away games, Real Sociedad became one of the foremost teams in Spain in the following campaign. They conceded just 20 goals and went invincible, going a record 38 matches undefeated in a streak that spanned the last six matches of the 1978/79 season and 32 matches in 1979/80. They gave defending champions Real Madrid an almighty scare before going down 2-1 to Sevilla in the penultimate round. It proved to be a heartbreaking defeat as the capital club sealed the title by a single point.

Real Sociedad's aura of invincibility lost some of its sheen in the 1980/81 season and they rarely rose to top of the table as they had done in the previous season. Their title bid seemed to have gone up in smoke when they dropped to seventh in February, after losing three out of the previous four matches, including reversals against title rivals Atlético Madrid and Barcelona.

What followed was nothing short of miraculous. Like a heavyweight boxer rebounding off the ropes, *La Real* strung together an undefeated streak and would not lose till the end of the season. They won eight of their remaining ten matches which included a 3-1 win over Real Madrid on 8 March 1981 thanks to goals from Diego Álvarez, Alonso and Zamora. It would prove to be a season-defining victory in the end.

In 1979/80, Ormaetxea's team had dropped to second after leading the table for most of the season. In 1980/81 they did the opposite, rising to top of the table for the first time towards the end thanks to a 2-0 win at Real Murcia. After dispatching Espanyol in the following round all they needed to do was to avoid a loss against Sporting Gijón in the last match. Ignacio Kortabarria calmed *Txuri–urdinak* nerves and gave them an early lead after seven minutes. Sporting Gijón legend Manuel Mesa then threatened to spoil the party, scoring twice to put the home team ahead. With Real Madrid winning their match and the clock running down, Real Sociedad were looking at another late season heartbreak.

Then came Zamora and the goal that immortalised him in the hearts of the Real Sociedad faithful. Level on points with Real Madrid, *La Real* won the title on head-to-head record in one of the closest finishes in the history of LaLiga. Real Sociedad's superior goal difference between the two matches against Real Madrid swung the pendulum in their favour.

Ormaetxea's Real Sociedad teams didn't play the sort of expansive, flair-filled football that is often associated with great Spanish sides. In goal they had Luis Arconada, one of Spain's greatest-ever goalkeepers who was ably supported by a stubborn defensive line consisting of Julio Olaizola, Genaro Celayeta, Inaxio Kortabarria and Alberto Górriz. Alonso was the lungs of a three-man midfield with Diego Alvarez and Zamora providing offensive threat. Although their strength was defence, Real Sociedad had a talented forward line led by Jesús María Satrústegui and López Ufarte. The former would end the 1980/81 season as their top scorer with 16 goals.

With each of their three strikers reaching double figures, Real Sociedad looked favourites to defend their title in the first half of the 1981/82 season. Eventually, they lost steam and a loss to Hércules in March saw *Txuri-urdinak* drop to third behind Real Madrid and Barcelona. Yet again, they finished with a swagger, winning four of their last five matches with title rivals

Barcelona falling in the final lap. For the Real Sociedad fans the second title was made sweeter by the fact that it was sealed with a victory over Athletic Club on the final matchday.

Athletic Club might have lost on that day but their time to shine had arrived. It came thanks to a man whose career at the Bilbao club was ended by an injury at the tender age of 24. Undeterred, Javier Clemente started coaching and eventually became an integral part of Athletic's brilliant youth system. He was still 32 when he was handed charge of the senior team in 1981. Using his experience of the academy, Clemente assembled a youthful team with an average age of below 25. Under him future legends like Andoni Zubizarreta, Ismael Urtubi, Santiago Urquiaga, Miguel de Andrés, Jesús Liceranzu and José Ramón Gallego became first-team regulars. Dani Ruiz-Bazán and Manu Sarabia were at the peak of their powers, forming a prolific striker partnership with able assistance from winger Estanislao Argote.

Clemente was a great admirer of the English style of football and was especially enamoured by Sir Bobby Robson's Ipswich Town. He even travelled to England to study them closely. Although common in England, his style of combining zonal marking with long balls was a novelty in Spain. Over the years, his Athletic Club side also developed the reputation for 'anti-football' thanks to a streak of violence that was interlaced with their often unbreakable defence led by 'Butcher of Bilbao',

Andoni Goikoetxea. It was a defensively rugged team but was also one efficient in scoring frequently. The knuckles-up approach also suited the 'us against the world' ethos of their fans.

Real Madrid or Barcelona, who had splurged in the summer on Diego Maradona, were expected to wrench the 1982/83 LaLiga away from Real Sociedad. Few expected Athletic Club to challenge for the title but they gradually rose to the top after outscoring every other team in the division. On 3 April 1983, Real Madrid delivered a body blow to their credentials with a 2-0 victory, but Clemente's side bounced back in style, ending Barcelona's title bid with a 3-2 win and then picking up a 2-0 win in the Basque derby.

Spanish football fans braced themselves for yet another photo finish when top-of-the-table Real Madrid travelled to relegation-battling Valencia while Las Palmas, also struggling to stay up, hosted Athletic Club. On 1 May 1983, Real Madrid hit the woodwork multiple times before being upset 1-0 by Valencia. Athletic, on the other hand, leapfrogged them with a convincing 5-1 win, sealing their first league title since 1956.

Athletic Club's bid to defend their league title floundered at the start of the 1983/84 season. Clemente had, by that time, developed a bitter rivalry with Barcelona manager César Luis Menotti. In a heated exchange of statements, Menotti accused Clemente's football of being destructive while *Los Leones'* boss hit back by calling the 1978 World Cup winner a 'hippie' and a 'womaniser'. The Argentine wrested the bragging rights when the sides met early in the season with Barcelona blanking Athletic Club 4-0. There was more bad news for the club from Bilbao when Goikoetxea was handed a lengthy ban after breaking Maradona's ankle with a vicious tackle. Without their defensive enforcer Clemente's side suffered as Real Madrid with *La Quinta del Buitre* – a side featuring stars like Emilio Butragueño and Manuel Sanchís – and Barcelona both looked like champions-elect. Athletic Club eventually recovered and rose to top of the table after suffering just one defeat in their final 12 fixtures.

On 29 April 1984 LaLiga's title race went down to the wire for the fifth consecutive season. This time, instead of two, all three teams – Athletic Club, Real Madrid and Barcelona – had the chance to win the league. During a see-saw 90 minutes each of the three teams were champions for a few minutes. Facing Real Sociedad, defender Iñigo 'Rocky' Liceranzu put Athletic Club ahead only to be pegged back by their rivals in the second half.

With the score tied at 1-1 and his team in danger of relinquishing the mantle of champions, Liceranzu again turned into an unlikely source of goals, nicking the 3,000th LaLiga goal in Athletic Club's history. The 2-1 victory was also sweet redemption for *Los Leones* as they paid back their derby rivals in the same coin as the final matchday of 1982. Athletic Club also won the Copa del Rey that season after an ill-tempered final with Barcelona which is best remembered for a free-for-all brawl at the end.

Athletic Club's double in 1984 proved to be the crowning moment of Basque dominance in Spanish football. The status quo was soon re-established as the clubs from Madrid and Barcelona gradually caught up with the Basque clubs. The duo embarked on infrequent cup runs, in both Spain and Europe, but other than Real Sociedad's gallant 2002/03 season neither have come close to challenging for the league title. Perhaps that failure makes the period from 1980 to 1984 all the more special. It was a period when the Basque clubs with their homegrown local players clashed swords with expensively assembled Real Madrid and Barcelona teams and emerged victorious with a hard-nosed efficiency that connected with their fans. These were teams filled with personnel who fought for their heritage, pride of the Basque nation and their shirts – a quality which has since become endangered.

THE RISE, FALL AND RISE AGAIN OF DEPORTIVO ALAVÉS

by Josh Butler *(@JoshisButler90)*

DELFI GELI soared into the balmy sky above the turf, his weary legs propelling him higher and faster than those around him, who stood as if with boots that had taken root in the pristine green. The darkness of the night expunged by the searing brightness of the floodlights of the Westfalenstadion, he rose to meet them, a modern Icarus, leaping where no man had leapt before.

Just like Deportivo Alavés had soared all season, higher and higher, ever closer to the glimmering grail of the UEFA Cup, so did Geli. Unflappable, unstoppable – until his head connected with the spinning ball and diverted it into the vacated goal to the sigh of a rippling net.

When Delfi Geli rose highest to nod home in the 117th minute of Deportivo Alavés's 2001 UEFA Cup

Final tie with Liverpool, it should have been a goal that crowned the most unlikely champions in football history.

Throughout their 80-year history, Deportivo Alavés had spent a grand total of six years in the Spanish top flight. This was a club more accustomed to living in the considerable shadow of their neighbours Athletic Bilbao and Real Sociedad. Alavés, based in Vitoria-Gasteiz in the Alava province of the Basque region, were not even what you could call a provincial force. For the most part, their existence had been spent oscillating between Spain's second, third and fourth tiers.

Yet, somehow, a mere three seasons after they had achieved a miraculous promotion from the Segunda División, conditions had conspired to propel this small, unassuming Basque club to the higher echelons of the sport – and an improbable UEFA Cup Final appearance.

At the turn of the century, Alavés had established themselves as a competitive outfit in LaLiga, under the shrewd stewardship of José Manuel Esnal. After avoiding immediate relegation back to the Segunda División in 1998/99, *Los Babazorros* shocked the Spanish footballing world by finishing sixth, a solitary point behind the mighty *Galácticos* of Real Madrid.

In a scarcely believable campaign, a side, whose most expensive purchase totalled €2m, rollicked home to a UEFA Cup berth, eight points ahead of the chasing pack, courtesy of victories over Barcelona, Atlético Madrid and fierce rivals Athletic Bilbao, as well as a

4-1 demolition of eventual champions Deportivo La Coruña. This was a period of upheaval in Spanish football; prior to the 1999/2000 season, the traditional duo of Real Madrid and Barcelona had won 14 out of the previous 15 championships. But with the tumult on the horizon in Catalonia and chaos reigning in Madrid, the conditions were ripe for the clubs outside of Spain's power bloc to exert their influence.

Alavés, deploying a 5-3-2 formation that extolled Romanian wing-back Cosmin Contra's considerable talents on the flank, became extraordinarily hard to beat. Across the 38-game season, they conceded only 37 goals, the fewest out of any club in LaLiga, and their reward was admission into the 2000/01 UEFA Cup.

What followed was an intrepid journey that saw Alavés make what was – and still is – their only appearance in a European final. After vanquishing the likes of Internazionale, Rosenborg, Rayo Vallecano and Kaiserslautern, their fairy tale was but a single match from becoming an unlikely reality.

With four minutes of extra time remaining, in a game that had seen nine-men Alavés come back from 3-1 to level the tie at 4-4, Delfi Geli would become immortalised for scoring the golden goal of this momentous UEFA Cup Final. The wing-back, who had spent the best part of the previous 116 minutes keeping the likes of Michael Owen and Emile Heskey quiet, had in fact risen to meet a Gary McAllister free kick, which he diverted beyond the helpless grasp of his goalkeeper

Martin Herrera to become the first man in European football history to settle a final with a golden *own* goal.

As Geli froze, his features locked in a rueful grimace, his team-mates descended into the various stages of disconsolation around him. Some threw their arms in the air, many stood dumbstruck, and others collapsed to the ground in sheer exhaustion. At the end of a gruelling contest, Liverpool celebrated as Alavés hearts were sundered with an almost audible crack, but lurking beneath this cacophony of jubilation and despondence was a sense that Alavés had come to the end of the road in more ways than one. Their journey had come to a screeching halt in both a literal and, more ominously, a figurative sense.

This was a side that should never have been in this position; a side brimming with previously undiscovered talent that would surely be picked apart in the coming months. Its overnight success would be exploited by the rapacious nature of Europe's elite. On that night in Dortmund, Alavés had been slain and it did not take long for the vultures to begin picking at the still-warm carcass.

After three consecutive top-flight finishes, equalling their longest-ever stay in the Primera División, José Manuel Esnal's carefully cultivated side was ravaged as a result of their over-achievements. First, top scorer Javi Moreno, the man who had plundered 22 league goals the previous season and who finished third in the race for the *Pichichi* to Raul and Rivaldo, was poached by AC Milan for €14m. Then, the incomparable Cosmin Contra, undeniably deserving of his inclusion in the 2001 UEFA Team of the Year, followed suit and departed for the San Siro the same summer.

Unfortunately for Alavés, the exodus began in earnest over the next two years. Goalkeeper Martin Herrera jetted off to Fulham, Serbian holding midfielder Ivan Tomic returned to AS Roma after his loan spell, and Jordi Cruyff – the man who had scored Alavés's all-important fourth goal in the 2001 UEFA Cup Final – headed to Espanyol. Then there was Hermes Desio, the Argentine holding midfielder who had represented the Alava club for six years, and long-time club captain Antonio Karmona – they both left the club in 2003. By the time the 2003/04 season came around, seven of that fabled night's starting XI were gone and Alavés found themselves once more in the surrounds of Spain's Segunda División.

A seventh-place finish in the 2001/02 season belied the turmoil that was gathering like darkened thunderheads on a rapidly approaching horizon. With such an enormous turnover of playing staff, consistency plummeted and Alavés slipped through the trapdoor of relegation with little more than a whimper.

Something of a false dawn followed, as the club returned to LaLiga two years later in time for the 2005/06 season but were unceremoniously relegated straight back into the second tier. Few familiar faces remained; of the 2001 class, only the grizzled centre-back Oscar Tellez and Argentine defensive midfielder Martin Astudillo still regularly turned out for the club.

By now, though, not even five years on from their zenith, Alavés were well on their way to approaching their nadir. During this time, the club had been sold to notorious Ukrainian-American businessman Dmitry Pietrman, whose repeated impositions saw the dismissal of three managers in the 2005/06 season alone. Unable to stomach his constant interference, successive managers came to loggerheads with the unpopular owner and, following clashes with the club's hierarchy, players and even the fans, Pietrman unsurprisingly abandoned Alavés in €25m of debt. Duly fleeing the country, he left Alavés teetering on the brink of bankruptcy. This instability, prevalent for years under his misguided stewardship, permeated every facet of the club, and plunged them into perennial relegation battles, the last of which they succumbed to in 2008/09.

For the first time in 15 years – and only seven seasons after they had come so close to clinching a remarkable UEFA Cup triumph – Deportivo Alavés were back in the third tier of Spanish football, once more residing in the unwelcome home they had tried for so long to escape from.

Much of their history has been spent battling the figurative demons of insolvency; Alavés have never been a rich club, and even their forays into LaLiga for the first time in half a century came with a tentative approach to the transfer market. They were frequently one of the division's lowest spenders during their five-year tenure around the turn of the century. Even with the much-needed cash injection provided from their European exploits and the sale of much of their top talent, it is a testament to the utter financial ruin wrought by Pietrman that Alavés were practically penniless, surviving on youth-team prospects, loanees and free transfers by the time they were acquired by former basketball star José Antonio Querejeta Altuna in 2013.

This was a period fraught with uncertainty, as Alavés lurched from season to season without clear guidance. At this step of the Spanish football pyramid, the leagues are divided into regions and many B teams of the Primera and Segunda divisións are prevalent. Despite finishing in the play-off places, it would be four years before Alavés escaped this regional sub-league and returned to the national scene.

Arriving at the club's time of greatest need, it was Altuna's Avtibask S.L. group that supplied the investment imperative to ensuring the club's survival. Their promotion back into the Segunda División a year later only added to the stability they had craved for almost a decade.

Where Alavés's first ascent to the penthouse of Spanish football had been swift, this time there was a patience born of experience that tempered the expectations of those within and surrounding this precarious club. Between 1994 and 1998, Deportivo

Alavés had risen from the third tier of Spanish football to the first by way of two promotions in four years. Now, however, the journey was to be undertaken with a sense of measured caution.

Four successive seasons in the Segunda División B eventually led to a further three successive seasons in the Segunda División before promotion was finally attained once more to the promised land of LaLiga. In 2016/17, a full 11 years since their last appearance, and 16 years since their most glorious achievement, Deportivo Alavés were once more rubbing shoulders with the likes of Real Madrid and Barcelona. These were bedfellows that Alavés had once enjoyed for the most fleeting of periods – five whirlwind seasons that flew by at a pace, a mesmerising blur of incredulous scalps and daring ventures into foreign climes.

This time, however, Alavés were prepared for their latest stay in LaLiga. There are no lofty ambitions this time around, born out of the serendipity of overnight success, but an awareness that this small club needs to be both financially and tactically shrewd if they are to remain in the Spanish top flight for longer than five seasons.

Thus far, the plan is working. The 2019/20 season marks Alavés's fourth consecutive campaign in LaLiga, and the club are on course to record four consecutive safe, mid-table finishes. Of course, remember this is Alavés and, lest anyone forget, they are a club that are staunchly synonymous with the unexpected.

In their first season back in LaLiga, they were without a win in their opening two fixtures, having drawn with both Atlético Madrid and Sporting Gijón, when they faced the stern prospect of travelling to the Camp Nou to face a Barcelona side bristling with stars. Though the likes of Messi, Suárez and Iniesta began the game on the bench, the *Blaugrana* still boasted Neymar, Rakitić and Paco Alcacer in their starting line-up, but were unable to answer Ibai's 64th-minute winner for Alavés.

Alavés would finish the season in a respectable ninth position, but their duology with Barcelona turned into an unexpected trilogy when the two met in the Copa del Rey Final on 27 May. Almost 16 years to the week, the blue and white striped men of Vitoria-Gasteiz found themselves once again competing in a major final. As with their previous excursion, the evening would end in disappointment, but, unlike before, where the peal of Liverpool jubilation invariably sounded the club's death knell, Alavés have not suffered a similar fate following the outpouring of Catalonian joy. Though the hurt of losing their first-ever Spanish Cup Final was keen, this was not an Alavés side built in the mould of its progenitor.

When first Alavés rose from the dark depths of the Spanish lower leagues, so immense was their exhilaration that they found out to their peril that there is only so high one can soar without sharing the fate of Icarus. The ashes that were left after the club's rapid descent lay cold and lifeless for a generation. Few ever thought Alavés would have forged the opportunity to soar again.

Now, Alavés have risen anew, tempered by their past mistakes, wary that over-exertion could lead once more to the forsaken plunge back into the gloom, and they glide now in the gentle zephyrs of LaLiga, knowing full well that to soar at this altitude will prove more beneficial in the all-important long run than flying once more too close to the sun.

SUPER DEPOR

by Ryan Plant *(@ryanplant1998)*

29 APRIL 2018: the mood at the Abanca-Riazor, Deportivo de La Coruña's 80-year-old home, is glum. The empty, blue seats amalgamate into one with the fans' home shirts and their blue, disconsolate faces. Their *Super Depor* are not so super any more.

Champions-elect Barcelona are the visitors. They need only a draw to clinch their 25th LaLiga title, and Depor need a win to avoid relegation to the Segunda División. Philippe Coutinho, a €160m signing, opened the scoring seven minutes in. Thirty minutes later, it's two. Lionel Messi volleyed home from Luis Suárez's chipped cross. As had become so typical of Depor's plight, they levelled to 2-2 with goals from Lucas Pérez and Emre Çolak and should have gone ahead, but thanks to Marc-André ter Stegen, they didn't.

With eight minutes to go, Messi danced around the Depor backline, bounced a pass off Suárez and finished calmly, as only he knows how, past Rubén. He then completed his 46th career hat-trick with a pass into the bottom corner, again from a Suárez delivery. Easy.

It was the first defeat in five league matches for Clarence Seedorf's Depor, which saw them drop into the second tier for the first time since the 2013/14 season. They were there in 2011/12, too. But this isn't a story about a typical yo-yo team, who flirt with the drop every season and, when they finally succumb to relegation, bounce back up.

Depor envied Barcelona that night. Their embarrassment of riches in every position, their notoriety everywhere they went and their slick, superlative attacking play made them undeniably the best team in the land. But there was a time when Barcelona begrudged Deportivo. So did Real Madrid. And Atlético Madrid. And AC Milan for good measure. This isn't a story about a team who skirmished with relegation every season until finally succumbing to the best team in Spain, either. This is a tale about the side who were the best team. It's one of the biggest falls from grace in world football.

In 1988, 30 years before Barcelona's visit to Galicia, Depor were in an arbitrary phase. Arsenio Iglesias, a former player at the club between 1951 and 1957, was tasked in the 1988/89 season with restoring the former glory of his playing days. His job, though, could have been much harder than it already was but for the composure of Vicente Celerio. In injury time on the final day of the 1987/88 campaign, he scored against Racing

Santander to earn an inestimably important 1-0 win; Depor's number seven had scored to avoid relegation to the Tercera División – the fourth tier of Spanish football – for the second time in the club's history.

Under the management of Argentine coach Alejandro Scopelli, Depor's side, including Iglesias, was one of the most exciting teams in Spain during the 1940s and 1950s. The squad boasted South American talent including Julio Corcuera, Oswaldo Garcia, Rafael Franco and Dagoberto Moll and was embellished by Luis Suárez, the only Spanish player to have won the Golden Ball.

After that, though, Depor gradually sunk down the divisions as Real Madrid's first *Galácticos* side took hold of Spanish, and indeed the world's, football competitions. They fell as low as the Tercera during the 1970s, though immediately came back up. But the club had bigger ambitions than that.

Celerio's goal is seen as a turning point in Depor's history. Indeed, it is hard to imagine Iglesias would return to the Riazor for a third time as manager with the club at its lowest ebb. Instead, he set about winning the *Branquiazuis* their first major silverware.

He came close. They fell to Real Valladolid in the semi-final of the Copa del Rey, which was a disappointment, but it promised a return to LaLiga, which eventually came, after an 18-year absence, at the end of the 1990/91 season, when they finished in second place in the Segunda behind Albacete.

Iglesias had done all he could – or so the powers that be at the Riazor thought. Marco Antonio Boronat was drafted in to replace him, for his second spell in charge. But he was ineffective, and Iglesias was ordained, for the fourth time, to resurrect the club. He did so again, negotiating a relegation play-off, beating Real Betis 2-1.

Iglesias addressed the core of his squad, much like Scopelli had during his playing days. He recruited López Rekarte, Adolfo Aldana and Donato from Barcelona, Real and Atlético respectively, scouted Bebeto and Mauro Silva from Brazil and promoted Fran to the first-team fold. This was far from a *Galactico* side – quite the opposite in fact, because Aldana had been shunted away by Real. It was instead a cohesive unit, fastidiously prepared and choreographed, to take down Spain's luminaries.

It was the blueprint for Deportivo sides that followed. In 1992/93 Depor were resurgent, occupying top spot in LaLiga for much of the season, before eventually dropping to third behind Barcelona and Real Madrid. They finished on 54 points, four off top spot, and Bebeto was the competition's top scorer with 29 goals, three more than Real's Iván Zamorano and nine more than Barça's Hristo Stoichkov. Depor were here to stay, surely.

The following season, they came even closer to their first LaLiga crown. They led for much of the season and went into the final day knowing a win against mid-table Valencia would guarantee the title. But it was not to be – again. With the score at 1-1 after 83 minutes, Nando won a penalty after being fouled by Valencia's José Serer. Miroslav Đukić had the chance to seal the win for Depor, but his spot kick was saved by José González. Barça were victorious, clinching first place for the fourth time in a row.

It looked as though Depor were set to remain at the top end of LaLiga but earn a reputation as nearly men in the shadow of Spain's great clubs. Indeed, during the 1994/95 season, Iglesias announced he would be leaving the club, and he could only muster another second-place finish in the league, this time behind Real. As is often the case today, if it isn't one, it is the other.

But that was until the Copa del Rey Final. Against Valencia, who had denied them a first LaLiga win a year previous, they were looking for their first Copa success at Real's Santiago Bernabéu. With the score at 1-1, though, the game was suspended after lots of water fell on to the pitch during a storm in the capital.

The two sides returned for the final seven minutes, and potentially extra time and penalties, three days later – but they were not necessary. Alfredo Santaelena's header gave Depor the win and caused pandemonium in the *Herculinos* sections amongst the 81,000-strong crowd. This time, the fourth time around, Iglesias had done all he could, but Depor hadn't.

A 3-1 defeat to Real Zaragoza in December 2019 left Depor at the bottom of the Segunda. A fan was interviewed on Spanish terrestrial television, and said his club was 'like a meme'. This was unimaginable only 19 years previously; not because the word 'meme' in 2000 would have been pronounced like the noise the Road Runner makes when escaping Wile E. Coyote, but because *Super Depor* really were super.

19 May 2000: Depor are top of LaLiga, ahead of Barcelona and needing only a draw to clinch the title. They had been here before though, and the nerves were palpable amongst the players, staff and the fans. But goals from Donato and Roy Makaay sealed a first league crown for the side which made A Coruña, with its population of only 180,000, the second-smallest city to house Spanish champions behind San Sebastián, where Real Sociedad reside.

Real and Barça had shared 14 of the previous 15 LaLiga wins. Since Depor's win, the Clásico rivals have won at least one of the domestic trophies on offer in every season. This was no mean feat for Depor but, even more impressively, it really did look like the first of many successes.

They started as they meant to go on: a 4-1 win over Alavés on the opening day saw them top of the league, alongside Louis van Gaal's Barcelona. But it was when the two sides met the following October that heads started to turn towards the Riazor: Makaay, a summer signing from Tenerife, notched two first-half goals as Javier Irureta's side saw off Rivaldo, Pep Guardiola and co by the odd goal in three.

Until then, Celta Vigo and Real Valladolid had also been in good form. And whilst the two Madrid clubs floundered (Real's manager, John Toshack, was sacked and Atlético were eventually relegated), a topsy-turvy season was expected, but not like this. Barcelona would lose their next four.

Fifteen matches in, Depor led the way in an all-Galicia top two ahead of Vigo. Real Zaragoza, Rayo Vallecano and Alavés completed a shock top-five rostrum. By the turn of 2000 they had a six-point lead over Zaragoza but, more importantly, they were seven ahead of Barça and 13 ahead of Real, who were reinvigorated under Vicente del Bosque.

Whilst Real's expansive squad – boasted by the signings of Iván Helguera, Steve McManaman and Nicolas Anelka – floundered, it was Depor's understated mixture of ferocity and flair that set the league alight. Makaay provided the lethal touch in attack, Victor Sánchez and Slaviša Jokanović were the midfield destroyers and the samba skills of Mauro Silva and Donato were intricate embellishments to the armour.

Irureta's squad were irresistible in 1999. But in the early epochs of the new year, they were anything but. If the seven-match winning run instigated by the Barcelona win was them at their best, then the five-strong away losing streak, including a 3-0 defeat to lowly Racing Santander, after the turn of the year was them at their worst.

It looked as though normality would be restored in LaLiga when out-of-sorts Depor met resurgent Real. It could only go one way, couldn't it? That's right: Depor notched five goals, which included a dazzling display from Djalminha, in a 5-2 win which they came away from angered at conceding two goals and dismayed at not scoring even more.

A 3-0 return defeat to Barcelona, just as Alavés were creeping up the table towards the summit, again looked like a severe reality check for Depor that would bring them back down to earth. But no, they scored ten goals in three successive victories after that, including a first in eight away trips to Sevilla.

Their return to form came at the right time as their rivals began to stutter. A five-match winless run ended Alavés's hopes, and Real endured three draws on the spin before exacting their revenge on Zaragoza with a 1-0 win. Then, Barcelona suffered two 3-0 defeats in a week to Real Oviedo and Real Mallorca, which left them far off the pace but still Depor's closest challengers. Irureta could see the finishing line, and van Gaal was still coming around the final corner.

But as Depor were getting close to the finish, they were limping. Defeats to Rayo and Celta allowed Barça to close the gap to the top with a win against Atlético, making the lead just two points with three games to go. A Barça win against Rayo would see them top, but Bobo, in one of the season's surprises, earned the Vallecas side a 2-0 win on their short journey to the

Camp Nou. Depor and Zaragoza drew 2-2, which gave them some breathing space. Valencia, after an incredible 2000, were suddenly in the picture, too.

Depor had won only once in six months on the road and stuttered to a 0-0 draw in Santander as Barça versus Real Sociedad also finished deadlocked. That meant a draw against Espanyol would be enough for the title. In retrospect, Depor could not have asked for a better match to contest for the occasion. Espanyol were mid-table with nothing to play for in LaLiga but did have a Copa del Rey Final to rest key players for whilst surely, secretly, hoping they would play a part in their neighbours' shock defeat.

Donato quashed any nerves after three minutes, heading his side ahead. The 37-year-old should have taken the penalty which could have won the title six years prior, but he was too nervous, making this goal extra special. After the final whistle, the Riazor faithful who had endured a day of despair in 1994 spilled on to the pitch to celebrate a famous win. A year later, they confirmed their status as the ultimate party-poopers by beating Real Madrid at the Bernabéu in the Copa del Rey Final with goals from Sergio and Diego Tristán, to spoil the *Blancos'* centenary celebrations at their own home.

Oh, how times change. Those same fans, at their own, emblematic home, were chanting 'Out with the board!' during the 2019/20 season. The decline was at first gradual: they finished second in the next two seasons and then third in the two campaigns that followed, with a squad including enviable talent around the midfield lynchpin, Juan Carlos Valerón.

They had some memorable moments in the UEFA Champions League, too. They defeated Manchester United, made a mockery of Arsenal and completed one of the competition's most stunning comebacks against AC Milan in 2004, recovering from 4-1 down in the quarter-final first leg at the San Siro by winning 3-0 at the Riazor to go through on away goals, before losing to eventual winners Porto in the semi-finals.

But football was changing. And Depor did not change for the better. Irureta's ideals were stale and outdated by his sacking in 2005, and Augusto César Lendoiro, the club's charismatic president who had previously spent ambitiously, could not match the new iteration of Real's *Galácticos*.

They finished eighth in 2004/05, 13th in 2006/07, 10th in 2009/10, and then 18th in 2010/11: relegation. The wound had worsened over the years; it became painful and, even when it began to look as though it would heal, it would just worsen. And it was Valencia – again – who struck the killer blow via a Roberto Soldado strike on 23 May 2011. Valerón, a star at the football palisades around Europe in Depor wins at the Bernabéu, Old Trafford, Highbury and San Siro, pulled his hair, cuddled by Donato at the final whistle. *Super Depor* were not super any more.

They immediately returned to the top flight for the 2012/13 season but were relegated again. These setbacks strangled the club's finances and saw them hit debts of over €170m on their return to the Segunda, and administration became a heavy burden on an already debilitated team.

There seemed to be redemption on the horizon when Tino Fernandez took the reins, halving the club's debts as a second immediate return in as many years was achieved. He was impatient, though: where managers were once given time to implement their philosophies, suddenly nine managers had gone through the revolving door at the Riazor's main entrance in five years. But Depor were surviving in the top flight – just about – for now.

That was until 2017/18. Seedorf, an uninspiring appointment who, ironically, would not have looked out of place in Depor's midfield at the time, oversaw only two wins in 16 matches. Depor were relegated and it was not to be third time lucky in the Segunda.

And their trajectory in 2019/20 was only one way: down. From mid-October to the turn of 2020 they sat rock bottom. Fernando Vázquez, the third manager this season, is overseeing a revival of sorts, but safety is far from secured. Twenty years ago, Depor were fighting with Barcelona for the LaLiga crown, way ahead of the Madrid clubs, but they are now simply aiming to make sure they do not finish 41 places lower at the foot of the second tier. The illness throes, the pain is menacing: will there be a miracle cure, or a sudden death?

THE HISTORY OF THE COPA DEL REY: A BELOVED COMPETITION MAKING ITS WAY BACK INTO THE FANS' HEARTS

by Kristofer McCormack *(@K_mc06)*

FOREVER TUCKED away in every quadruple, treble or double is a domestic cup. The Coppa Italia, the Coupe de France, the FA Cup. Though all famed awards, few in Europe enjoy as rich a history as Spain's Copa del Rey. The history of the King's Cup runs almost parallel with the story of Spanish football, having started in the summer of 1902 and continuing in different forms to the present day. In that time, teams, figures and finals have come to characterise an ever more colourful competition and, with that colourful history reappearing in 2020, there hasn't been a better time to recount its epic tale.

Football in Spain began life outside the Basque city of Bilbao during the late 1880s and 1890s. It was popularised by English workers and students and played in abandoned bullrings and fields outside the country's big cities. Come the 21st century, a handful of football clubs existed, competing exclusively against other local sides in a series of friendlies and regional championships. Among those clubs was Madrid FC (Real Madrid), who at that stage had already established themselves as one of the premier sides in the Spanish capital.

Keen to test his team's pedigree among the nation's finest, club president Carlos Padrós was among the first to suggest a national cup competition. Padrós's suggestion was quickly made a reality with the help of former club member, Luis Bermejillo. When not playing football, Bermejillo was the accountant and close friend of Count de la Quinta de la Enrajada. He suggested to the Count to host a football tournament at the Madrid Hippodrome, to commemorate the coronation of the new king, Alfonso XIII.

In the summer of 1902, the Copa de la Coronación was contested by five teams: Madrid, Barcelona, Espanol (now Espanyol), New Foot Ball Club (Madrid-based club) and Vizcaya, the sole Basque side in the competition. Vizcaya had been made specifically to play in the cup and was a mixture of players from Bilbao's two biggest clubs, Athletic Club and Bilbao Football Club.

Ordinarily fierce rivals, the two clubs united to win the first cup, beating Barcelona in the final. Carlos

Padrós refereed the showpiece; however, he was the match's only Castile representation as Padrós's own club lost the very first Clásico 3-1 in the semi-finals.

The success of the Copa de la Coronación encouraged the young Spanish football authorities to continue the competition; the following year the Copa del Rey (the King's Cup) was played for the first time.

Following Copa success and a dip of interest in Bilbao, Vizcaya became a permanent fixture, changing its name to Athletic Club Bilbao. The new club entered the cup as defending champions and this time defeated Madrid FC 3-2 in the final. The challengers initially opened a 2-0 lead but collapsed in the second half, much to the annoyance of the Madrid Hippodrome. The game made such an impression on some disgruntled Madrid club members that they decided to form their own club in honour of Athletic Bilbao, Athletic Club de Madrid.

The first two decades of the Copa del Rey saw Athletic Club establish themselves as the cup's dominant force. Between 1903 and 1920, the Basques reached 12 finals, winning eight of them.

They retained their title in 1904 without playing a game as their potential challengers refused to agree on a time and place to play a semi-final. In 1905, they lost the final to Madrid FC, who would win a further three titles (a record). It would be 1910 before Athletic Club would win another Copa. That year saw two Copas played due to a disagreement over who should organise the competition. Traditionally, the holders of the Copa del Rey organised the Copa. This changed in 1909 with the the founding of the Real Federación Española de Fútbol (RFEF), who took over organising the tournament in 1910. A split occurred between RFEF member clubs and the rest, resulting in two cups being played.

Athletic Club won Real Sociedad's competition, beating the holders and organisers in the final (Barcelona won the RFEF version). In 1911, some clubs complained, ironically, about the foreigners in Athletic Club's squad. In response, *Los Leones* dropped their best player and still won the competition. That same year, they signed teenager Rafael Moreno. The inside-forward would go on to become known as Pichichi and inspired the Northerners to a three-in-a-row between 1914 and 1916, scoring a hat-trick in the 1916 final against Madrid FC.

The Spanish national team travelled to France for the 1920 Olympics, reaching the semi-finals much to the surprise of the world press. By the end of the tournament, Spain's two standout players were both playing for Barcelona, namely Ricardo Zamora and Pepe Samitier. Having won the 1920 title, Barcelona would win four more cups including the 1928 final against Real Sociedad, the first to be broadcasted on radio.

The next year was one of great change for the cup. On the pitch, a national league was founded, beginning a shift in prestige from the Copa to the new Liga. Off the pitch, Spain was beginning to take a significant turn politically. The military dictatorship of Miguel Primo de Rivera ended, and a Republican government was elected, resulting in the exile of the royal family and the Copa del Rey becoming the Copa del Republica.

Amongst all this change, Athletic Club became Spain's first league and cup double champions in 1930. Three more followed into the 30s, equalling the record for most Copas won in a row. In 1936, the first-ever Clásico Copa Final was played in Valencia. Madrid raced into a 2-0 lead; however, Barcelona scored to set up a tight finish. In the end, former Barcelona keeper, Ricardo Zamora, would be Madrid's hero making a spectacular save in the final minutes of the match to win the cup.

Mere months after that final, the Spanish Civil War broke out, leading to all RFEF competitions being suspended. Nonetheless, football persisted, regional leagues appeared and were competed by a handful of teams that had the resources and peace to do so. In 1937, the Copa de España Libre (Free Spain Cup) was founded. Four teams (Girona, Levante, Valencia, Espanyol) played each other twice in a first-round group stage with the top two sides qualifying for the final. Levante topped the pack and defeated city rivals Valencia to lift the cup. For club sources, this victory is Levante's sole top-flight title; however, the RFEF refuse to recognise the trophy, despite the campaign gaining popular support in recent years.

The 1943 Copa semi-final perhaps remains the most infamous match in the competition's history. The controversy started in the first leg of the semi-final which Barcelona won 3-0. Both sides finished the game feeling aggrieved with the referee. Madrid had complaints about all three Barcelona goals while *Blaugrana* fans had whistled the referee for allowing Madrid's rough style of play.

In the week leading into the second leg, Spanish nationalists worked up the Madrid public over the atmosphere and refereeing of the second leg, encouraging them to go a step further in the return leg. Fearing the growing tensions, the Barcelona president sent a letter to Real Madrid pleading that they appeal to their fans to remain calm. Madrid released a statement claiming, 'The more incorrect one set of fans' behaviours, the less sporting to try and emulate it.' The statement then went on to say that the club wasn't trying to 'curb *Madridelinos* enthusiasm', taking some bite from the opening words.

Before the match, home fans met in bars to collect whistles; former Madrid president Ramón Mendoza was 16 at the time and claimed the noise was 'extraordinary'. Away fans had been banned from travelling to the game, leaving just the team to handle whistles that were so loud one Barcelona player thought his 'ear drums would burst'. It took only five minutes for the Barcelona penalty area to fill with coins as the away keeper had to avoid his line as it would have put him within the range of fans armed with stones.

Come 30 minutes, Madrid were 3-0 up and a man up. By half-time, the home side had an 8-0 lead and would have been further ahead if it wasn't for the linesman twice ruling them offside. According to most sources, Barcelona refused to play the second half, at which point a Spanish government official or military general entered the dressing room and threatened the players with jail if they didn't carry on playing. Three more Madrid goals came in the second half alongside a Barcelona consolation to make the final score 11-1, the biggest Clásico victory in the fixture's history.

Forgotten in the tale of political intrigue and controversy of the 1943 semi-final was that Real Madrid lost the eventual final. Atlético Bilbao (forced to change their name under the new regime) staged a massive upset at Chamartín in Madrid to collect the cup from an undoubtedly bitter General Francisco Franco. In that side was Agustín Vicandi. The cup was his first success with Bilbao, but it certainly wouldn't be his last. A talented forward, Vicandi would captain Athletic Bilbao to seven Copas, the most cups won by a single player. Three of them came on the trot (1943, 1944, 1945) before a Real Madrid back-to-back broke the Basque hogemeny. In the 1947 quarter-finals, Vicandi would score a record eight goals against Celta Vigo as Bilbao dismissed their Galician opponents 12-1.

As if such firepower wasn't enough, Atlético also had the legendary Telmo Zarra in their ranks and it was the eventual Copa all-time top goalscorer that won the 1950 edition, scoring four goals against Real Valladolid in the final. In 1958, Atlético Bilbao won their 20th Copa title. Across nearly 50 years, the Basques, in some form or another, had competed in nearly half of all the Copa finals played and had lost just seven of them. That the club has played a grand total of ten finals since then and won just four (the last coming in 1984) is startling and speaks to the shift that took place in Spanish football with the arrival of Alfredo Di Stéfano.

The next bookmark moment in Copa history came during the 1968 Copa del Rey, also known as the Bottles final. The tournament had been largely dominated by the Madrid teams during the 1960s; however, the 1968 final pitted Real Madrid and Barcelona. The *Blaugrana* took the lead via an own goal in the sixth minute and held on to their lead to seal their 16th Copa title, much to the fury of the Real Madrid players and fans whom maintain that the referee purposefully denied them two clear penalties. So frustrated were they by Antonio Rígo's performance, the home crowd started throwing bottle caps at the referee, littering the pitch while Barcelona celebrated their win. The game led to glass being banned from stadiums in Spain.

Two years later, the two met at the Camp Nou for a quarter-final. Real Madrid led 2-0 from the first leg; however, they conceded first in Barcelona and seemed set to concede another when possession was won back and Amancio Amaro and Manuel Velázquez broke away on the counter. Velázquez was taken down, rolled into the penalty box and won a spot kick. When one of the Barcelona players complained, he was sent off and, with Amaro's later conversion, Barcelona lost all hope of a comeback. Real Madrid went on to win the Copa that year, a crucial victory as it meant they qualified for the European Cup after finishing outside the top three in the league. Barcelona, meanwhile, were left aggrieved and believing bigger things were a foot than a refereeing mistake.

Entering the 1970s with controversy swirling in the air, one can only imagine the uproar the 1979 Copa del Rey caused. Enjoying a golden generation in the second division of Spanish football, Real Madrid reserve team Castilla defied all odds in 1979/80 to reach the Copa del Rey Final. On their way they played three LaLiga sides including the mighty Athletic Club. Not wanting to miss the occasion, Real Madrid's senior side also reached the cup showpiece at the Santiago Bernabéu. The two sides had been paired for a match on three occasions during the tournament; however, due to the ridiculous rules of the Copa, they were only allowed to play each other in the final. The senior team won 6-1 with both teams celebrating the cup victory.

In 1984, Athletic Club reached the Copa del Rey Final in search of a historic double. In their way was Diego Maradona's Barcelona. Due to their contrasting approaches, Barcelona and Athletic Bilbao had developed quite a rivalry in the mid-1980s. In reflection of this, the final had been prefaced with some strong words from both club managers. 'Barcelona is prepared to respond to determined violence with the same violence,' Barça manager César Menotti claimed, and he wasn't lying.

Athletic Club won a physical affair 1-0; however, it's the unsavoury scenes following the final whistle that are remembered, with a massive brawl breaking out on the pitch. Everyone was involved, from players to club officials and fans. One of the Bernabéu fences at the Athletic Club end even collapsed in the carnage with medical staff from both clubs rushing around amongst the chaos treating the injured. Menotti left Barça soon after while Athletic Club manager, Javier Clemente, remained for a few years before also leaving.

Since the 1990s, the Copa del Rey has slowly descended into a bit of a farce. From teams like Celta Vigo, Real Betis and Real Zaragoza featuring and winning cup finals, in the 2010s every final featured either Real Madrid or Barcelona. Between 2015 and 2018, Barcelona won four consecutive Copa titles, each in comprehensive fashion. In 2018, the club swept Sevilla aside 5-0, the biggest margin of victory in a final in the competition's history.

Despite Valencia's victory in 2019, it was quite clear heading into the new decade that change was needed. Hence, starting for the 2019/2020 season, the two-legged knockout games were done away with up until the semi-finals and the number of sides present in the competition upon entry of the first team was booted up from six to 75. This has led to some highly entertaining clashes and an unlikely final of Real Sociedad versus Athletic Club, 110 years after both sides met in a final for the first time.

The Copa del Rey has changed faces several times since it began all those years ago, going from the premier competition in the country to a runner-up prize as of late. One would hope that the changes made in 2019 revive the cup's reputation and put it back among the top prizes in Spain once again.

THE IDENTITY OF FOOTBALL ON THE SPANISH ISLANDS

by Will Gittins *(@WillGitt)*

GEOGRAPHY PLAYS an important role in Spanish football. Spain was once a peninsula of competing kingdoms and those factions are still visible in the nation's football clubs today. Real Madrid, the country's most successful side, are a beacon of the capital's riches. Their 'Real' (royal) moniker was bestowed by King Alfonso XIII and they were described by Fernando María Castiella, the Minister for Foreign Affairs under General Franco, as 'the best embassy we ever had'.

Barcelona, on the other hand, fly the flag for the region of Catalonia. They trumpet their 'More Than a Club' mantra, and a number of *Blaugrana* legends have turned out for the unofficial Catalonian national team.

Athletic Club employ a *cantera* policy which ensures that they only sign players who are native to or were trained in the Basque Country, a fairly small area on the French border.

All football clubs are shaped by their surroundings but some far more than others. There are a handful of clubs who are indelibly linked to their remote situation, whose unique identity could not be replicated in any other city or town in Spain. Away from the mainland and far out at sea, these are Spain's island clubs.

The Balearic Islands

The most famous and successful of the offshore outfits is Real Mallorca. Founded in 1916 by Adolfo Vazquez, the club was initially named Alfonso XIII Football Club after the then King of Spain. His Highness was clearly impressed and later that year King Alfonso honoured the club with the title Real Sociedad, to leave the rather clunky name of Real Sociedad Alfonso XIII Foot-Ball Club. A linguistic nightmare for any would-be ultras looking to craft a chant.

They were renamed Real Club Deportivo Mallorca (RCD Mallorca) from the 1949/50 season and success followed. Back-to-back promotions in the late 1950s saw them reach the Primera División, the precursor to LaLiga, for the first time in their history. Promotion brought a switch to professional status as they became the first full-time club from a Spanish island.

However, Mallorca struggled to really establish themselves at the top table. Burdened by the extra travel expenses and greater wages demanded by players who relocated to the island, by the 1970s their financial situation was precarious. Debts spiralled after relegation to the Tercera División and issues reached a head in the 1977/78 season when they were unable to pay wages, with some reports claiming that players locked themselves in the changing room in protest. That season, Real Mallorca were relegated to the fourth tier of Spanish football for the first time in their existence.

It took a series of intelligent managerial appointments and greater investment but by the mid-1980s Mallorca were back in the top flight. However, it wasn't until the turn of the millennium that they really began to put the Balearic Islands on the European footballing map. In 1997/98, new manager Héctor Cúper guided them to a fifth-place finish in LaLiga. The Argentinian steered them to third the season after and, although he would soon leave for the bright lights of Valencia, his stewardship inculcated a new sense of self-belief – both in the players and the fans.

Another third-place finish in 2000/01 saw them finish eight points clear of Barcelona and qualify for the Champions League. Under Gregorio Manzano they morphed into exciting cup specialists, fielding a 21-year-old Samuel Eto'o alongside the maverick talents of Walter Pandiani up front. Although they were inconsistent in the league, their 2002/03 Copa del Rey triumph (featuring a 4-0 thumping of Real Madrid along the way) will live long in the memory.

Cup success and forays into Europe marked the early 2000s as the most successful period in Real Mallorca's history and the best spell enjoyed by any of Spain's island clubs. Arnau Riera, a Mallorcan midfielder who left the island in 2001 to sign for Barcelona, remembers the impact that this side had on Spanish football:

'Mallorca were the flagship club for Palma, Mallorca and the whole of the Balearic Islands,' he explains. 'People in Menorca and Ibiza and Formentera supported Mallorca and were proud that we could put up a LaLiga team to compete with the best.'

Their place amongst the nation's best seemed secure but, once again, they were hamstrung by financial disparity as stars like Eto'o and Diego Tristán were plucked by LaLiga's vultures. Until 2016, Spanish clubs were allowed to sell their own broadcasting rights on an individual basis, unlike the collective deals struck by the Premier League. So while LaLiga's big boys were able to cash in on their enormous global appeal, sides with smaller followings received far less. In the 2011/12 season, for example, Real Madrid made over €140m from television income; lowly Granada received just €12m.

This has since been rectified with LaLiga clubs now receiving a more even split, but island teams still struggle to match the commercial power of clubs on the mainland. Real Mallorca, despite sustained top-half finishes, were unable to cement their position at the top table of Spanish football. They will hope that, under the ownership of American investor Robert Sarver and former NBA star Steve Nash, they may finally be able to compete financially with those on the mainland.

The Canary Islands

Mallorca's location has undoubtedly affected the club, but they are practically metropolitan compared to some of the Spanish league's more remote competitors. Just off the northwestern coast of Africa, over 1,300km from Europe, sit the Canary Islands. A Spanish territory since the 15th century, the Canaries are home to UD Las Palmas.

Organised football in the Canaries originated on the island of Gran Canaria in 1910, when Pepe Gonçalves founded Real Club Victoria after falling in love with the game during his time studying in England. A number of other teams began popping up around the island and as interest swelled a brave move into the Spanish national competition was mooted. However, for these clubs on a distant island of less than 200,000 people, competing against the mainland's established clubs seemed like a pipe dream.

That was until Don Manuel Rodríguez Monroy, Vice President of the Regional Federation, suggested that a single club could represent Gran Canaria on the national stage. His idea was to merge five of the island's biggest existing sides – Club Deportivo Gran Canaria, Atlético Club de Fútbol, Real Club Victoria, Arenas Club and Marino Fútbol Club – to form one team. Negotiations were understandably tricky but, on 22 August 1949, the new club named Unión Deportiva Las Palmas was founded. The aim was not only to boost football in the region, but to prevent their most talented players feeling the need to move to the mainland to further their careers. From the very beginning, Las Palmas were a response to their isolated location.

Starting in the lowest of the Spanish national structure's three tiers, UD Las Palmas secured back-to-back promotions in their first two seasons in existence and remain the only club to have achieved that feat. In that first season in the top division they were, unsurprisingly, more successful at home than on the road. In fact, all but one of their 22 points were earned on Gran Canaria. They beat Valencia and Sevilla at home but finished second from bottom and were relegated.

A decade later, under new manager Vicente Dauder, the club was again promoted and in 1964 began its longest uninterrupted period in the top flight. They finished second behind Real Madrid in the 1968/69 LaLiga season and the islanders' prominence in Spanish football was also recognised at international level. Las Palmas players Paco Castellano, Germán, Juan Guedes and Tonono all represented holders Spain in the 1968 European Championships, while one-club man Tonono would go on to captain the national team.

However, while they had proved themselves the equal of some of Spain's top clubs, their isolated location prevented them from competing on a commercial basis. They were dependent on the money they received from playing in LaLiga and so relegation to the Segunda División was a disaster for the club.

In both 1988 and 2002 their fall from the top tier was swiftly followed by another relegation as the club's budget was slashed and the squad stagnated. Relegation to the Segunda B in 1992 saw the club lumbered with a debt of €3.6m, while in 2004 their relegation forced them into bankruptcy proceedings. On both occasions they were saved by donations from those on the island, like Miguel Ángel Ramírez, a local businessman who bought the club in 2004 to preserve Gran Canaria's only major sporting institution amid debts of over €60m.

Throughout its history Las Palmas' island identity has been a blessing and a curse: a commercial and logistical burden that is lightened by the strength of support on Gran Canaria. Theirs is a very rare situation in the vast scope of global football, but one with a unique appeal for those lucky enough to experience it.

Matt Rayns, a Midlands native, first moved to Gran Canaria in 2010 for a work placement with travel company TUI. He was a Derby County fan by birth but stumbled across UD Las Palmas by accident during his time on the island and caught the bug.

'On arrival in Gran Canaria I didn't speak a word of Spanish,' he says. 'But I used football as an interest to help me learn the language.

'After leaving the island in September 2014, I kept an eye on the club from afar: results, league tables, reading match reports and following fan-run groups. I watched the play-off promotion win from my home in Derby and had decided that I had to go to a game at one of the big two on the mainland.'

That play-off victory came in 2015, a nerve-wrecking victory over Zaragoza with an 85th-minute winner sealing their return to the top-flight. Desperate to experience *Los Canariones* in LaLiga, Matt flew out in October that year to watch them face Real Madrid at the Santiago Bernabéu. He felt a connection to those on that distant island and was struck by how the Spanish style of supportership intensified around the island club.

'The big thing in Spain is the peñas,' he says, referring to the bar-based fan clubs that act as a proxy for the matchday experience. 'The street alongside the stadium, Calle Fondos de Segura, is where you find bars like La Arrancadilla, Ca' Jorge and Bar Willy – all teeming with fans. The local group, Ultra Naciente, are responsible for the atmosphere and any *tifo* activity. For the *Derbi* matches against Tenerife and the play-off games in 2014 and 2015, the streets are a sea of yellow and blue; songs are heard loud and proud and you get a great sense of their passion.'

El Derbi Canario features the Canary Islands' two most successful teams, and pits the two largest islands against each other, hundreds of miles from Spain's other professional sides. In terms of securing local bragging rights, UD Las Palmas vs CD Tenerife has few equals.

Sergio Maccanti is a lifelong Las Palmas fan and vice president of one of the club's largest peñas: *Amarillos por el Mundo* (Yellows Around the World). Speaking to him it is clear that this single fixture stands above all others:

'Well, this is a group of islands, you know? Rivalry is part of the game. When in the same division, CD Tenerife and UD Las Palmas play in two leagues: one against the rest and [another] against each other in a fight for pride. Our *Derbi Canario* is a huge celebration of football in the Canaries and far beyond the seas.'

Strangely, these matches are fairly infrequent. Of the 67 seasons in which both have played in the national system, they have spent just 18 in the same division. Games between the two are therefore viewed as a rare treat and Matt's first experience of the *Derbi* in 2018 remains one of his fondest memories of the club.

'I was invited along by a photographer who is a good friend of mine and a journalist from the island-based paper, *Canarias7*. I was given an all-access tour of the stadium and even made the front page the next morning, with the headline 'From Derby, for the Derbi'. I met the first-team squad and coaching staff and was presented with a signed shirt by the club captain. I felt honoured.'

The score finished 1-1 that day, a contentious penalty securing a point for Tenerife at the death, but for Matt it marked a next step in his devotion to the club. He now runs Las Palmas fan pages on Facebook and Twitter that provide coverage of the club for *Los Canariones* supporters all over the world. His presence is so appreciated by those within the club that in 2019 Nicolas Ortega, the vice president, invited him to his box for a game against Albacete. Sitting there in the Estadio Gran Canaria, drinking his favourite beer (the locally produced Cerveza Tropical), Matt watched his adopted side run out 3-2 victors.

*The connection between Matt and UD Las Palmas reveals an important detail about football on the Canaries, and about island football in general. In these isolated regions football is a thread that unites people and offers a connection to the mainland and the world beyond. They are less a club *for* the island, but a club *of* the island: representing its people on a global stage.

From RCD Mallorca putting the Balearic Islands on the footballing map, to the aptly named 'Yellows Around the World', football is a vessel for island identity. In Sergio's words: '[We are] the expression of an extraordinary feeling of love and unity around a major social institution in a tiny island far, far away from the mainland … a very special way of understanding football for thousands of yellow fans all over the world.'

THE CAUTIONARY TALE OF MÁLAGA

by Rahul Warrier *(@rahulw_)*

IN LALIGA, life below the big duo of Barcelona and Real Madrid is a scrap. While teams such as Atlético Madrid, Sevilla and Valencia usually finish near the top, the financial gulf between the El Clásico rivals and the rest means that there are always opportunities to make your way to the 'best of the rest' class. The difficulty lies in maintaining the position once you make it. It's always easy to chase a pack, but more difficult to hold off competition. With Málaga, however, they found it difficult to contain their own dreams. Flying high like Icarus with dreams of silverware, the wings eventually melted off, casting them into the cold sea of the second division.

After relegation in 2005/06, it took Málaga two seasons to make their way back to the first tier. They finished eighth in their first season back under Antonio

Tapia, but then found themselves going backwards the following season. Málaga won just seven games, the joint-lowest in the league, and drew 16. Their inability to turn those draws into three points saw them finish 17th, just one ahead of Tenerife and Real Valladolid (albeit with a much better goal difference). The Andalusians found themselves with some extraordinary streaks: having beaten Atlético Madrid 3-0 in the season opener, their next win would come in their 15th game. They also enjoyed a nine-game unbeaten run (with two wins). Nevertheless, they were lucky not to go down having not won any of their final 11 games.

Safety was the precursor for greater changes in the club: economic problems saw president Fernando Sanz sell his majority stake to a member of the Qatari royal family. Sheikh Abdullah bin Nasser Al-Thani took over Málaga for the price of €36m inclusive of the club's debt. He was announced as the president on 28 July 2010. Juan Muñiz, meanwhile, was sacked on account of the poor finish the previous season and was replaced by Jesualdo Ferreira. The Portuguese coach had become the first to win the Primeira Liga in three consecutive years at Porto, but he had left despite a Taça de Portugal triumph salvaging a poor 2009/10 season. After four years, he moved to Málaga.

Unfortunately, it didn't go to plan. Málaga were in 17th after nine games, with just two wins and a draw. A six-game winless streak in the league saw Ferreira receive the sack early, a sign of Al-Thani's ambitions.

That was further strengthened by the appointment of the next manager. Manuel Pellegrini was presented as the new coach on 5 November and watched from the stands as they lost 1-0 to Espanyol. He took charge in the Copa del Rey fourth-round replay against Hércules CF, winning 3-2, and then beat Levante 1-0 in his first league game.

Pellegrini had a strong résumé prior to Málaga. A one-club footballer for Universidad de Chile, his management career saw him take charge of a number of South American teams. After winning titles at LDU Quito, San Lorenzo and River Plate, he took over Villarreal in 2004. In his five seasons, the Yellow Submarine finished third (2004/05) and second (2007/08), while they were foiled by Arsenal twice in the Champions League: the 2005/06 semi-final and 2008/09 quarter-final. On the back of this, Pellegrini was appointed as manager of Real Madrid in the summer of 2009, overseeing significant investment in Kaká and Cristiano Ronaldo amongst others. Yet, round of 16 defeats in the Copa del Rey and the Champions League didn't help his cause, and he was replaced by José Mourinho despite a record 96-point total seeing them finish three behind Barcelona.

Ironically, Pellegrini's last game for Real Madrid was against Málaga. He took the Andalusians to a solid 11th place that season, but his work next season proved to be of greater significance. After great investment in the squad in the summer of 2011, Pellegrini took Málaga to their highest-ever finish: fourth, with 58 points. While miles away from Real Madrid and Barcelona, this achievement secured qualification for the Champions League play-offs. The previous season had seen €22.5m invested into the likes of Sebastián Fernandez, Salomón Rondón, Martin Demichelis and Jülio Baptista, but Al-Thani spent more than double that sum to back Pellegrini. It was a statement of intent. If it wasn't enough, Fernando Hierro was signed as director general.

Santi Cazorla was the 25-year-old starring transfer, moving from Villarreal after five league goals and nine assists. For €20.7m, he was the club's most expensive signing. He was well supported by an array of talent, such as Jérémy Toulalan, Nacho Monreal, Joaquín, Diego Buonanotte, Joris Mathijsen and Carlos Kameni. More intriguing though were the additions of two other attacking players: Ruud van Nistelrooy and Isco, both at opposite ends of their careers. It was a well-balanced squad in terms of age profile, and it is no wonder that they stole a march ahead of other similarly placed Spanish teams.

Despite a 2-1 loss to Sevilla in the opening game, Málaga started the 2011/12 season well with four wins and a draw in the first six games. That was followed by three consecutive losses, but the Andalusians were largely able to stay in the run. This was despite a horrid run in December and January that saw a six-game winless streak. A strong March kept them in the run for Europe, and despite losses to Barcelona and Atlético

Madrid in the 36th and 37th league games, Málaga secured fourth with a 1-0 win over Sporting Gijón – typically a Rondón header from a Cazorla corner. Both players were cornerstones of this team: the Spaniard scored nine, assisted six and played the most minutes; 21-year-old Rondón had 11 goals and four assists. Isco, the 19-year-old starlet signed from Valencia, scored and assisted five. Things weren't as smooth, though, due to the club's irresponsible financial conditions. It is difficult to comprehend how an owner, apparently flushed with money, could struggle with finances. After all, it was he who announced the club's budget would be €150m in a bid to challenge Barcelona and Real Madrid. But when Pellegrini had asked for winter signings, he had only gotten goalkeeper Carlos Kameni on a free. The proverbial tap seemed to shut, salaries were paid late, and this only fed into the discontent. The absence of the president in the city didn't help either.

They didn't always play as a team; no surprise given the number of additions in recent years. Pellegrini struggled to take charge of the side at times, with a lack of character permeating through the squad. Nevertheless, they managed to finish in the top four, pushing structural issues to be dealt with at a later stage. Cazorla, van Nistelrooy, Rondón and Mathijsen threatened to complain against the club post-season, and while the club agreed a deal to prevent automatic relegation to the Second División B, it came at a cost. All four left: Cazorla moved to Arsenal for less than he was bought for, a price Pellegrini called a gift. Rondón moved to Rubin Kazan, Mathijsen left on a free to Feyenoord, while van Nistelrooy retired. The clubs Málaga dealt with the previous summer complained about not receiving full payment, while Fernando Sanz demanded money for the sale of the club.

A transfer ban (later reversed) was imposed for their missed payment to Osasuna for Monreal. Spanish clubs and financial difficulties weren't a new story, but this was a club being backed externally. Al-Thani's representative Moayad Shayat helped to restructure the club, trying to let them stand on their own. Eventually, their European qualification was not denied to them. Earnings were embargoed however, with both Hierro and director Antonio Fernandez departing, and the prospect of signings looking slim.

Despite this off-pitch tumult, Málaga managed to get off to a flying start in their next season. After going up 2-0 at home in 34 minutes in the Champions League qualifying round versus Panathinaikos, they closed that and the away tie with ease (a 0-0 draw). That put them in a strong group, with Zenit St Petersburg, Anderlecht and Milan. Despite this, they were unbeaten in their first ten games of the season – six league wins, two qualifiers as well as a 3-0 home win versus Zenit and a 3-0 win at Anderlecht. They also beat Milan 1-0 at home, while drawing the remaining three games, ensuring they finished unbeaten in the group stage.

In the round of 16, Málaga fell to Porto in the first leg, with João Moutinho giving the Portuguese the advantage. Isco and Roque Santa Cruz helped the Spanish team win the home leg 2-0 though, taking them to the quarter-finals. They were drawn to Borussia Dortmund, Bundesliga champions in the previous two seasons. A 0-0 tie in the first leg at home sparked hope that they could do the improbable. Joaquín put them ahead in the second leg after 25 minutes, and while Robert Lewandowski equalised before half-time, Eliseu made it 2-1 with eight minutes of normal time to go. As it stood, Dortmund needed two goals to overcome the away-goal advantage. And then everything went awry.

In the 91st minute, Neven Subotić knocked the ball towards Marco Reus who converted to make it 2-2. Two minutes later, a Lewandowski cross bounced around the box – with four Dortmund players offside – eventually falling to Santana – also offside – who tapped in from a yard out. The referee blew the whistle after the four minutes of injury time was up, despite the two goals, and Málaga was desolate. Poor officiating stole what was to be the crowning achievement for the Andalusians: a semi-final against Real Madrid. Al-Thani left his rage to Twitter, urging for a probe and blaming 'racism', but it was too late.

Málaga were dropping in the league table at the same time, and four losses in the last eight games saw them drop to sixth. That included thrashings on the road at Valencia (5-1), Real Madrid (6-2) and Barcelona

(4-1). They finished nine points off a Champions League place. But it didn't matter. The club fell foul of UEFA's Financial Fair Play rules and were banned from European competition for at least one season for unpaid bills. The second year of their European ban was eventually waived, but it didn't matter either. That was the highest they would finish in the league.

Al-Thani had only started with his gradual asset-stripping. It wasn't a surprise. Isco left for Real Madrid for €27m, Toulalan was off to Monaco, while Joaquín (Fiorentina), Demichelis (Atlético Madrid) and Javier Saviola (Olympiacos) were some of the other departures. Pellegrini, meanwhile, left for Manchester City. Bernd Schuster, ironically another former Real Madrid manager, took over, but they finished 11th and he was sacked. And the cycle continued. Pellegrini came in to buy Willy Caballero the following season. Meanwhile, Málaga's reliance on free transfers and loans continued.

The team Javi Gracia took over was not the same Málaga that Al-Thani promised, or the one that were close to the semi-finals. Despite the lack of investment, Gracia struck gold. The *cantera* had produced a crop of talented youngsters. Sergi Darder, Samu Garcia, Juanmi and Samu Castillejo all came through the academy and were regular starters. They were well supported by Ignacio Camacho and Ricardo Horta, both of whom joined the club at the start of their careers. Málaga finished five short of the Europa League spots in ninth place. They looked well placed for a revival.

And then the youngsters were sold. Both García and Castillejo moved to Villarreal, Darder moved to Lyon, while Juanmi was sold to Southampton. Nordin Amrabat, another first-teamer, was sold to Watford in the winter. It placed Gracia in a difficult situation, forcing him to rebuild the team once again. He had built his midfield around Darder, and was left compromised, forced to start over again. That season saw plenty of turnover and a difficult start to the campaign. After 13 games, Málaga were bottom of the league. But Gracia managed to get the team to start picking up points. They eventually finished eighth, far away from Europe, but well clear of relegation in a tight mid-table.

Gracia left for Rubin Kazan after that season, enticed by the significantly higher wages. Juande Ramos came in but was sacked by December; his replacement Marcelo Ramos was given just over two months before getting the sack too. They finished 11th, including a 2-0 win over Barcelona. But this was the sign of a club drifting without any plan. Any semblance of a sporting project had all but gone; 2017/18 was the season it all came to a head.

Twenty-eight losses in a season does not make for pretty reading. Málaga spent the entire campaign in the bottom three, winning and drawing five each. The die was cast when Camacho, Pablo Fornals and Sandro Ramírez were sold. With the lack of investment, the time had come when penny-pinching was no longer going to work. The loss of a number of experienced heads, who either retired or left the club, didn't help either. José Recio, the academy graduate, was the only player from Pellegrini's time. Málaga got desperate in the winter window, signing a number of forwards on loan. Their highest goalscorer, Diego Rolán, had five goals and it was nowhere near good enough. And so Málaga finally met their end, a mammoth 23 points away from safety.

After a decade in the top tier, they were back in the second division. While they bounced back from their previous relegation in two seasons, that seems less likely now. They made it to the promotion play-offs in 2019, losing to Deportivo La Coruña 5-3 on aggregate. They had finished five behind second-placed Granada, having lost both games to them in the season. If there was any hope of swift redemption, it had been dashed. The financial difficulties could have been allayed with a return to LaLiga, even if significant investment wasn't possible. Things look dire now.

Shinji Okazaki, of Leicester City fame, signed for the club on 30 July 2019. The club announced they would be releasing him on 3 September 2019, as the transfer window closed. Why? The salary limit prevented the club from registering him, and so he left without playing a competitive game. It might be the defining embarrassing moment for the club, but especially for the indifferent ownership. Regret over the Al-Thani takeover will be widespread, and fans might even sacrifice their Champions League heroics for stability.

The debt hovers over the club like an albatross. On the opening day of the season, Málaga somehow won with just nine players on first-team contracts. Coach Victor Sánchez had to fill the team with youth players; then as two first-team players went down injured, he had no room to make proper changes – federation rules state that teams have to forfeit if they have less than seven first-team players on the pitch. It was a sorry situation.

As the club declined, the state of the club could be viewed from Al-Thani's Twitter account. The feeling is that Al-Thani decided to channel his funds towards his other many projects. Some say he grew frustrated that his other projects weren't progressing and/or they weren't getting enough TV money. It feels as though Al-Thani was a man for the good times and had no patience to build the club. In 2012, club officials approached Marbella-based BlueBay Hotels to ask whether they wanted to help fix their finances in return for a stake in the club. Al-Thani would own 51 per cent of this new company, with BlueBay the rest. This new company would own 97 per cent of the club's stake that Al-Thani owned.

In 2014, the Qatari businessman announced that the deal never materialised, then evicted the hotel chain from club premises. He transferred the shares in the holding company to one owned by him alone. They reacted by launching a civil case in 2015 to force Al-Thani to comply with their agreement. Al-Thani has stalled ever since by filing his own case, but in March

2020 the court ruled in favour of BlueBay. His other investments in the area have fallen short too. In essence, he has milked the club, leaving them in a difficult place.

Málaga are a cautionary tale of foreign ownership selling dreams to a middling club, only to leave them high and dry. When a club relies on a foreign owner for investment, they leave themselves at the mercies of the whims of an unknown person. Al-Thani had money initially, but his interest in the club waned rapidly. More importantly though, the club has been hung out to dry financially. What might be more gutting is the fact they had a strong core of youngsters coming through the years: responsible fiscal management might have seen greater consistency.

It would be a huge shame to see the club become an answer to a quiz question, to become just another story. Yet their trajectory points towards the third tier. It's a sorry state, especially for the fans. It was a meteoric rise; everybody had a good time, but once the party ended, Málaga found themselves alone, having to clean up. More than anything, the club deserve stability. The fans deserve it. One can only hope they can find it away from the spotlight.

HOW MARCOS SENNA BECAME ONE OF SPAIN'S FINEST MIDFIELDERS

by Brad Jones *(@bradjonessport)*

BETWEEN 2008 and 2012, the Spanish created a breathtaking template of football perfection with a squad that oozed finesse and flair to provide all of football's greatest aesthetic pleasures game after game. Looking at the talent Luis Aragonés and Vicente del Bosque had at their disposal is like a who's who of the world's best in their respective positions at the time, none more so than their masterful midfield. Ask any football fan of this period, irrespective of knowledge and experience, to name Spain's midfield arsenal and they would breeze through four or five at least. But one man's mention may, more often than not, slip through the cracks.

Born and raised in São Paulo, Marcos Senna never threatened to be a world-class footballer during his formative years. It wasn't until the age of 25 that his career really came into fruition. After showing glimpses of his capabilities during spells at Corinthians and Juventude, he earned a move to Brasileiro Série A runners-up São Caetano, where he helped them go one further in reaching the final of the Copa Libertadores in his first season. Despite defeat to Paraguayan side Olimpia in the final, Senna's ability to conduct a team from the sitting midfield role was evident but understated to say the least. Not understated enough, however, for Villarreal to bypass the opportunity for his signature in 2002.

Upon his arrival in Spain, Senna's true potential was unknown by many. He wasn't known as a distinctly tough tackler, hard presser or sublime passer, and so he was never going to explode on to the scene and take one of the world's best leagues by storm. After making 16 out of 19 appearances during the first half of his debut season, he didn't feature in LaLiga for 13 months before returning to the starting line-up in March 2004; a two-season period which saw Villarreal climb from 15th to eighth with an insignificant contribution from Senna. Though, as the summer of 2004 began, the Brazilian was given a breakthrough in the form of new coaching arrival, Manuel Pellegrini.

Throughout his career, Senna steered clear of the spotlight due to his ability to master skills undetectable to the untrained eye: reading passes before they were played and covering space available for onward runs before they were made. But if one man could appreciate

Luis Aragonés, the beloved coach who would lead Spain to their first international trophy in 44 years and begin an era of dominance on the international scene.

Alavés put in a valiant effort in the UEFA Cup Final of 2001, but fell to Liverpool.

Many believe the Copa del Rey has lost its charm, but could it become the tournament that Spain adores once again in the near future?

The island clubs have had a huge influence on football in Spain – the battle from the Canary Islands between Tenerife and Las Palmas is a cherished fixture.

Losing a Champions League quarter-final in the dying seconds must have been heartbreaking, but the worst was yet to come for Málaga.

The Spanish conquerors of 2008 were full of superstars; Marcos Senna was an unlikely icon.

The Welsh dragon at the Anoeta: John Toshack took Real Sociedad to new heights.

At the peak of their powers: Deportivo La Coruña made a mockery of Milan in the Champions League.

Luís Figo and Rui Costa were two incredible talents in a generation of big names in Portugal.

Born in Mozambique but a legend in Portugal: Eusébio's legacy is always remembered in the Iberian nation.

Winning the Europa League Final in 2011 is the highlight of André Villas-Boas's career thus far.

Nobody expected Boavista to go so far, but at their best, they won the league and got a chance to play against Manchester United in the Champions League in 2001.

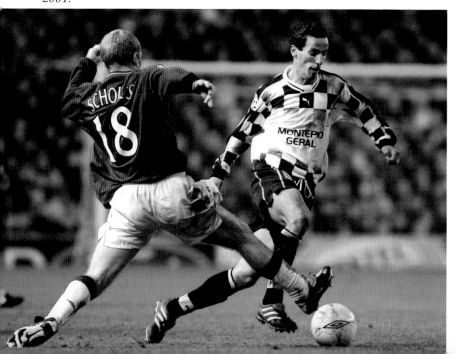

Jorge Jesus is one of the most innovative coaches in Portuguese football and has enjoyed success wherever he has managed.

Champions of Europe: the crowning moment in Portuguese football.

SC Braga: the humble club looking to break the norm in Portuguese domestic football.

Bobby Robson's influence goes far in both Iberian nations.

Senna's talent, the midfielder's own impressive career from then on proved that it was the visionary Chilean.

Pellegrini's first season as manager instilled a heightened sense of belief into a club that had hovered around mid-table since promotion in 2000 and a player whose progression had been equally stagnant of late. Going forward, very little was left to be desired about Villarreal. Juan Román Riquelme and new signing Diego Forlán were entering their prime amidst the emergence of teen sensation Santi Cazorla. It was the preceding anchor, the glue between defence and attack that Pellegrini was missing, and in Senna, it soon became clear that he had found his man.

Playing in a possession-based team, Senna would rarely maraud forward, but his importance lay in enabling their more creative outlets to do so with immaculate service and little positional consequence. He was crucial from a defensive and offensive standpoint – reflected both in Riquelme and Forlán combining for 43 league goals and the resultant record third-placed finish and Champions League qualification they achieved.

The following season, Spanish defender Quique Álvarez may have been wearing the armband for the most part, but Senna was the captain of the Yellow Submarine, the orchestrator of a blossoming team that continued their momentum into a spectacular Champions League run. During their first-ever endeavour in Europe's most prestigious tournament, Villarreal began their campaign with a 4-2 aggregate win over Everton to qualify for the group stages; the Merseyside club went on to be the first of four British teams they faced along the way.

Pellegrini had never managed in the Champions League, nor were his players experienced in European competitions with the exception of a few. But having the presence of Senna instilled a sense of confidence and freedom throughout the rest of the team – almost as if the middle third of the pitch was enclosed under a forcefield, controlled impeccably by the South American.

As the group stages got underway, it soon became apparent that Villarreal could not unlock their opponents in the fashion they could last season but, fortunately, that frustrating feeling was mutual. Manchester United arrived first, boasting Paul Scholes, Wayne Rooney, Cristiano Ronaldo and Ruud van Nistelrooy but offered little to no threat going forward in a 0-0 game that set the tone for the rest of the group.

The ensuing cagey affairs played straight into Villarreal's hands, particularly when Senna was on the pitch. No other team had a gatekeeper for the back four like him, and when push came to shove, he had a level of in-game intelligence and tactical nous that few possessed, which, more often than not, saw him carry his side through to marginal victory.

They finished the group, consisting of Benfica, Lille and United, undefeated and in first, scoring just three and conceding once in their six fixtures. A quite extraordinary run of low-scoring results which was testament to their solidarity and ability to wear down their opponents, draining every last drop of danger they posed. Defensively, they were organised and drilled with inch-perfect precision. Protected by Senna, known for rarely trying anything out of the ordinary, just playing the game simply, subtly and sensationally, they never looked fazed or under pressure, regardless of the opposition. What Senna brought was much more than football ability: he was an asset that every, even the very best teams, desperately needed, and his calming demeanour was infectious.

In the round of 16, Villarreal faced Scottish giants Rangers either side of an international break. After two more suitably tense affairs, Pellegrini's men scraped through on away goals after drawing both matches, and as they progressed into unprecedented, unfathomable territory, it was the week in between the two legs that was perhaps even more ground-breaking for Senna's career. This was the international break which saw him make his debut for Spain having been granted citizenship just months before. The *Seleção's* loss was Spain's gain, and with a new generation of exciting young Spaniards coming through the ranks, it was a Brazilian descendant that would prove to be the missing piece of the jigsaw.

Nevertheless, his attentions were still solely on Ol' Big Ears; all else was put on hold as the trophy shone just five games from his grasp. Next up was a trip to San Siro to face Roberto Mancini's Inter Milan, who would go on to win a domestic treble that season but couldn't find a way past Senna and co over two legs. Once again, the midfield general's unconventional yet functional style of play was the embodiment of his team's system. Despite losing 2-1 in the away leg, the Spaniards remained composed needing a single goal to progress, and if their previous Champions League encounters were anything to go by, it was clear that this had become somewhat of a speciality.

Two weeks on from another famous night at El Madrigal, Villarreal were into the semi-final of the Champions League having scored just eight goals in ten matches. Only Arsenal stood between them and the final, and after a narrow 1-0 defeat at Highbury, the tie was perfectly poised as the carnivalesque atmosphere inundated the city one last time.

For the majority of the game, the hosts executed their game perfectly, frustrating Thierry Henry, Cesc Fàbregas and the like before plugging away at the Arsenal defence. Senna was at the heart of everything as they continued to fight until the very last minute, when they were awarded a penalty. A golden opportunity to take it to extra time with momentum and the home crowd behind them. Up stepped the ever-dependable Riquelme. Saved.

Villarreal were out, but the sense of accomplishment and pride around the city on that unforgettable night meant so much more. The reason this season is spoken of in such detail is not only their outstanding achievement to exceed any conceivable expectations, but because it encapsulates Senna as a player, as a man, as Villarreal. Much like the infamous 2005/06 squad, Senna is not remembered for his moments of magic, nor his world-class ability, but for his commitment, his ever-presence and his consistent ability to perform under any circumstances. Qualities that went on to be tested on numerous occasions throughout his Villarreal tenure. For now, though, he continued to savour his prime years as he entered into his thirties.

By the start of the following season, Senna had established himself in the Spain squad after featuring in three of four World Cup games before they were knocked out by France in the round of 16. The Spaniard was still a key part of Pellegrini's plans after the club fought off interest from Manchester United to retain his signature, but his international career, much like the start of his Villarreal career, didn't quite take off as smoothly as he would have hoped.

Luis Aragonés tinkered with almost every aspect of his team following an underwhelming World Cup performance, and a befittingly flat domestic campaign saw Senna soon fall out of favour. He featured just once in the next 19 international fixtures over the next 18 months, but his resilience and distinct expertise kept him on Spain's radar, and after an unprecedented 2007/08 campaign, the midfielder soon fell back into the fold.

As time went on, Villarreal's devastating duo of Riquelme and Forlán were replaced by Giuseppe

Rossi and Robert Pires alongside the additions of Joan Capdevila, Pascal Cygan and Diego Godín. Having arguably lost their best two players of the last two seasons, the 2007 summer transfer window proved to be high-risk, very high-reward.

Though he was still occupying a defensive midfield role, Villarreal's newly appointed captain became more involved in an attacking sense, combining with his new team-mates seamlessly from the get-go. Villarreal finished the season in second, behind Real Madrid and ten points clear of Barcelona, and whilst their new signings made an undoubtedly huge difference, the key to their free-flowing football, their cohesion and their strength of character fell at the door of their midfield maestro once more. His consequent call-up to Spain's Euro 2008 squad despite not featuring in any qualifiers came with little surprise, even relief, to some.

Aragonés's men were in exceptional form heading into the tournament with six world-class midfielders to choose from, not including Senna. You'd struggle to find hotter competition for a position anywhere throughout football history and, yet, it was Mr Villarreal, the man with one Spain start in two years, that got the call.

Up until this stage in his career, Senna's role as an enabler, an orchestrator of magnificent football was a role he had become synonymous with. Only now, he was enabling David Silva, Andrés Iniesta and Xavi. To touch upon a previous point, Senna wasn't known as a distinctly tough tackler, hard presser or sublime passer, but he was all of the above to a formidable level, and the subsequent service and space he provided for their tantalising trio set poetry in motion as the Spanish blitzed everyone to claim the European throne.

It was hardly a coincidence that Spain's golden era was ultimately born out of Senna's introduction as a starter. Nor was it a coincidence that he went on to win all of his last 21 international matches. With Senna, Spain's blueprint for world domination was complete. Being such a late bloomer, however, Spain knew that they would soon need a replacement for the 32-year-old. Fortunately enough, that soon arrived in Sergio Busquets. The Yellow Submarine, on the other hand, would eventually begin to sink in ill-preparation of Senna's decline.

Villarreal were still a force in Spain and Europe for the next three seasons, one with Pellegrini in charge before B team coach, Juan Carlos Garrido, took over the reins after Ernesto Valverde's brief, forgettable spell at the helm. Senna's involvement was as crucial as ever during the 2008/09 season, when the Chilean led them to a Champions League quarter-final before the Gunners got the better of them once more, alongside a fifth-placed LaLiga finish.

In Garrido's first two seasons in charge, the veteran midfielder still featured heavily; even in spite of a four-month injury setback in the 2010/11 season, they weren't rid of him just yet. His perseverance was pivotal not only as they secured Champions League football once more, finishing fourth whilst reaching a Europa League semi-final but, more importantly, in the wake of Garrido's departure and the resultant fallout. Garrido was the first of three Villarreal managers during a season that saw almost a decade of tireless work to become an established outfit in Europe torn apart. After losing all six of their Champions League group games and suffering similarly bad form in LaLiga, the Spaniard was sacked in December as the Yellow Submarine plummeted to the second tier in the months that followed.

The subsequent state of the club following relegation and the consequent summer of upheaval was catastrophic but hardly unexpected. However, everything they achieved in the ten years prior, the memories of their most successful era, remained in the form of Senna. As everything else crumbled around him, he prevailed only to strengthen his legacy and his loyalty to Villarreal even in such adversity. Testament to his greatness as a player and as a man, Senna led Villarreal to promotion at the first time of asking in his final season with his beloved club, only to return three years later to become a club ambassador, thus solidifying a special club-player relationship that has almost emerged as an archaic concept in modern-day football since.

Growing up in Brazil, Senna was never expected to be a world-class footballer, and some would argue he never earned that status. Those people, looking at his career in hindsight, would surely stand to be corrected. He's not Xavi, he's not Iniesta, he's not Riquelme, but remove a player of Senna's calibre and neither are they. He is not held in such high regard when comparing him to his aforementioned midfield partners, but featuring so frequently, for both club and country, in their respective most successful ever periods is a clear indication of his importance.

His ever-presence, his loyalty, his rarely recognised yet extraordinary talent should and will forever be remembered.

REAL SOCIEDAD'S
WELSH DRAGON

by Dan Parry *(@DanParry_)*

THE BASQUE coastal town of Zarautz is a true football place. Its beach holds an annual tournament in which some of the region's finest players have tested their skills over the past 50 years. And, if you take a stroll along the beach, you could bump into any number of the Basque Country's footballing royalty. Legendary Athletic Club keeper José Angel Iribar was born here, so too was full-back Yuri Berchiche. Mikel Arteta owns a house here not far from former Spain, Athletic Club and Real Sociedad manager Javier Clemente's place.

Walking around the town, you might also encounter one of the region's favourite foreigners. A certain Welshman who spent a total of nine years as Real Sociedad manager across three different stints. His name is John Benjamin Toshack. Known in Spain as John Benjamin due to confusion around his middle name, Toshack became *La Real*'s manager in 1985. It wasn't his first time in the coastal city, though. In 1975, he played up front when Liverpool faced Real Sociedad in the UEFA Cup. He lined up against players he would one day coach, such as Luis Arconada who was making his debut. Ten years later, Arconada would help Toshack win the Copa del Rey.

As a player, Toshack was a serial winner. At Liverpool he formed a lethal partnership with Kevin Keegan, helping the Merseyside club win a total of seven major trophies in the 70s, including two UEFA Cups. He left Liverpool in 1977 to become player-manager at Swansea. They got promoted three times in the space of four years between 1978 and 1981, going from the old Fourth Division to the First Division. It was an unprecedented rise for the club. He initially established Swansea as a force in the top division too.

They finished sixth in their first season but couldn't maintain the momentum. Swansea then suffered back-to-back relegations, leading to Toshack's resignation in March 1984. After leaving Swansea, Toshack decided to look abroad.

His first foreign post was with Sporting CP in 1984. Toshack lasted less than one season in Lisbon, but it was a pivotal period in his managerial career. It was his first taste of an overseas league and he grew as a coach whilst learning to deal with different styles, tactics and mentalities.

By all accounts his Sporting side were decent. They only lost twice in the league under the Welshman and finished second. The problem was that Porto were spectacular. They ran away with the league title and won the European Cup the following year. In his autobiography, *Toshack's Way: My Journey Through Football*, the Welsh manager said his time in Lisbon 'opened the door to the rest of my life, it was the beginning of an eye-opening experience'. It sparked an odyssey in which Toshack managed 11 clubs in eight countries and worked as an international coach for Wales and Macedonia.

The peak of his managerial career occurred in Spain. He coached Real Madrid twice, Deportivo La Coruña and Real Murcia. With Real Madrid he won the league, even broke records for goals scored in a season, and at Depor he picked up the Supercopa.

But his biggest impact came in San Sebastián at Real Sociedad. Toshack made an indelible mark on the club during his first stint between 1985 and 1989. During that period, the Basques won the Copa del Rey in 1987 and were runners-up in the league and cup in 1988. The trophies along with his eccentric personality made the Welshman an enduring icon at the Basque club.

Toshack arrived at Real Sociedad in the summer of 1985, becoming their third manager in the space of ten years. At the time Real Sociedad had a strict 'Basque-only' policy – the same as neighbours Athletic Club. This also applied to the coaching staff. Toshack was the club's first non-Basque coach since Harry Lowe in 1935. On top of that, Toshack replaced beloved coach Alberto Ormaetxea, the man who had led the *Gizpukoanos* to consecutive titles in 1981 and 1982. Suffice to say, Toshack's appointment wasn't universally accepted among fans. Well aware of the lack of enthusiasm surrounding his arrival, Toshack set about endearing himself to the locals. He bought an apartment overlooking the city's *La Concha* beach and threw himself into life in the Basque Country.

On the pitch, Real Sociedad were in a rut. The club had gone off the boil and complacency had seeped in after years of dominance. The average age of the squad had increased considerably, and an overhaul was required.

As Toshack alluded to in his autobiography, success combined with a distinct identity led the club to falter. Ormaetxea and his staff were *La Real* born and bred. Understandably, the previous management trusted the older players who'd done so much, but as a result lost the ability to see their failings. The system designed to protect the club had been spiked by its own success. So, the club looked outwards to Toshack, as it would 'be easier for an outsider to dismantle what had been so successful and begin again'. Of course, this was not a simple matter at a club that could only sign Basques. Toshack had to reinvent the side and reignite the club's stagnating youth system.

Toshack began his project to rejuvenate the *Gizpukoanos* from within. He kept Ormaetxea's assistant manager and former Real Sociedad player Marco Antonio Boronat for his own backroom team. He didn't make any drastic changes to the Real Sociedad squad in terms of personnel, but he did promote six youth players to train with the first team three times a week.

The 1985/86 season got off to the worst possible start. Captain and Spain keeper Luis Arconada suffered a devastating knee injury against Celta Vigo in the first match. He would be out of action for the entire campaign.

Arconada was the 'Governor' as Toshack put it. In front of him were two young and uncommunicative centre-backs, Alberto Górriz and Agustín Gajate. Arconada was constantly marshalling them – Toshack lost his most authoritative figure at the back. Twenty-year-old keeper Agustín Elduayen replaced the veteran but struggled to impose himself. Ten games later Elduayen came down with appendicitis, leaving only third-choice keeper, José González, who got off to a terrible start with a 5-1 loss to Terry Venables's Barcelona.

As a remedy, Toshack reverted to the 3-5-2 system that served him well at Swansea. He converted commanding defensive midfielder Juan Antonio Larrañaga into a sweeper and placed him between the talented but quiet defensive duo. The side needed to adjust to '*El sistema Toshack*' but eventually the change of tactics paid off. A key moment came when Real Sociedad defeated Barcelona 3-2 at the Camp Nou in March. It was part of a run of four wins in their final five games, which also included a 5-3 victory over Real Madrid in the last match of the season.

Arguably, the most significant episode of that season, and John Toshack's entire time in San Sebastián for that matter, came after Real Oviedo knocked Real Sociedad out of the Copa del Rey in November. An *El País* column reported how Toshack, incensed by a perceived lack of professionalism in the defeat, 'punished' his players by forcing them to head back to San Sebastián at 04.00 am and not the planned 09.00. The players also had to participate in an extra training session upon getting back to the city.

News of the move spread fast. The press were waiting for Toshack as the coach got back to the Basque Country. The media shoved cameras and microphones in his face, demanding an explanation as to why the players had been woken up so early. Toshack's response earned him a lot of respect: 'There are a lot of people in San Sebastián, who pay for their season tickets, who have to wake up at four in the morning and earn a living,' he told the local press. 'The fishermen out there on their boats in the Bay of Biscay trying to catch enough to feed their families, the dock workers at the port moving cargo all day long.'

The Basque Country is proud of its reputation for being down-to-earth and hard-working. His justification affected everyone, especially his players, who were perhaps frightened of receiving a similar punishment in the future. Real Sociedad wouldn't lose a Copa game for another two years. At the end of the 1985/86 campaign, Real Sociedad finished seventh in the league. Toshack had settled in, put his systems in place and got a firm grasp of the club. The world hadn't been set alight, but it was a step in the right direction.

The next season, nicknamed 'Liga del play-off' for its complicated post-season play-off system, would see Toshack's *La Real* side play a total of 54 games. In the league, there was no major improvement. But Toshack made history in the Copa. With a bit of help from Arconada, Real Sociedad won the competition for the first time since 1909.

The initial rounds saw Real Sociedad take on sides from lower divisions. With the notable exception of a 10-1 drubbing of Real Mallorca B, most of the games were settled by a goal or two.

The first real challenge for Toshack's team came in the semi-final against Basque rivals Athletic Club. They drew the first leg at Real Sociedad's home ground, the Atotxa. It was a turgid affair; *Mundo Deportivo* described the game as a 'failure for anyone turning up with the hope of watching good football and an interesting battle'. Matters were complicated further for *La Real* in the 47th minute, when striker Loren Juarros got injured. The forward had been brought on as a substitute for injured midfielder Javier Zubillaga. Toshack was out of replacements and Real Sociedad played the rest of the game with ten men.

Unlike many others, Toshack attempted to draw positives from the game and immediately set about playing mind games with Athletic Club. In his post-match interview he said that 'Athletic Club's lack of ambition would be key to winning the semi-final'. For Toshack, not conceding the away goal when playing an entire half with ten men showed that Real Sociedad could get a result at San Mamés.

And he was right. The match at San Mamés was another 'tight affair'. But the big break came in the 25th minute. Gorriz helped a corner on its way to young forward José María Bakero, who outleaped his marker to put Toshack's side ahead 1-0. Real Sociedad had the away goal and went through to the final at Real Zaragoza's Estadio La Romareda.

'*No pasa nada, tenemos a Arconada!*' was a typical Real Sociedad fan chant from the 80s, which in English roughly translates as: 'Don't worry, we've got Arconada!' It was an ode to the prowess of their idol. The goalkeeper who was now into his 11th season with the club was a master of the penalty – he saved 12 of the 58 he faced in the Primera División. It was he who would invoke this superpower to guide his club to glory in the final.

The final was played on an insufferably hot June day, with temperatures reaching up to 36 degrees celsius. *La Real*'s opponents were Atlético Madrid, the side led by Luis Aragonés, who knocked out city rivals Real Madrid in the semi-finals.

As Toshack put it, the final 'ebbed and flowed'. Neither side could gain the upper hand. Real Sociedad dominated the opening passages, midfield maestro Roberto López Ufarte ran the show for his club and put *La Real* in the lead in the ninth minute. But, Atlético responded in the 24th minute, when a sensational one-two put Jorge Da Silva through on goal. Ten minutes later, Txiki Begiristain received the ball in the box on his left foot and cut back inside before dispatching a shot into the top right corner. Fifteen minutes from full time Atlético hit back again. This time, Julio Salinas crossed the ball to an unmarked Rubio, who put it to the left of Arconada.

When full time came around, the players were exhausted. The heat had drained them, they had nothing left in the tank and the final crept into penalties. Real Sociedad didn't miss one; all four takers scored with ease. However, the true hero of the day was Luis Arconada; the veteran goalkeeper got down low to save Quique Ramos's effort, thus giving Real Sociedad their first Copa del Rey since 1909.

In a 2018 interview with *El Diario Vasco*, Toshack said the final was the 'most memorable night of my career'. In his autobiography he describes the crowds of people who travelled from all over the Basque Country to San Sebastián in order to greet the team coach. The importance of what he'd achieved and what it meant to the province of Gipuzkoa dawned on him. At the time of writing, Real Sociedad still haven't won a major trophy since. The victory cemented Toshack's place in the club's history books and made him a legend.

He almost repeated the feat one year later. In June 1988, Real Sociedad faced Barcelona, who were now led by Aragonés. This time around, however, Aragonés and Barcelona got the better of Toshack and his players, winning 1-0. Real Sociedad also finished as runners-up in the Primera División, their best finish in the competition since the days of Ormaetxea.

At the end of the 1988/89 season, Toshack left. Real Madrid made him an offer he couldn't refuse. This wasn't the end of the story for *La Real* and John Toshack. The Welshman would return to San Sebastián twice more in his career. He wasn't even gone for long. Although he won a league title in Madrid, he rubbed the press and the board up the wrong way and by 1991 he was back in Gipuzkoa.

But his exit in 1989 was the start of a new era for Real Sociedad in a different sense. The club lost several of its best players to rival clubs – especially Barcelona and Athletic Club – after Toshack left. So, Real Sociedad abandoned its Basque-only policy. The first non-Basque player to arrive … a Liverpool striker named John.

They say that Real Sociedad still model their transfer policy on John Aldridge. They look for character, substance and work ethic above all else. The players might not be Basque, but they should at least display the values Basques hold dear; they should be Basque in spirit. The historians and journalists got the wrong John. San Sebastián fell in love with John Toshack first. It was the fiery Welshman who paved the way for foreigners at Real Sociedad.

Reference:

TOSHACK, J. *Toshack's Way: My Journey Through Football*, deCoubertin Books, 2018

PORTUGAL

PORTUGAL'S GERAÇÃO DE OURO

by Nathan Motz *(@nathanmotz)*

WOULD YOU believe Portuguese football ever existed before, and independent of, Cristiano Ronaldo's unprecedented feats of conquest? It is forgivable to believe Portugal were irrelevant before the coming of football's Alexander the Great. Portugal's qualification for the 2000 European Championship was only its fourth major tournament finals appearance since the 1966 World Cup presided over by another legend of Portuguese football, Eusébio. But the turn of the millennium earmarked a historical change in not only the fortunes of the small Iberian Peninsula nation, but a shift in the balance of power and influence in the modern European game itself.

After 2000, Portuguese actors – players, managers, and agents – proliferated in leagues across the continent, raised trophies, established legacies, became superstars, and finally attained national team glory which was thought beyond reach for a nation so small.

But as in every historical or fictional tale of emergent transformation, a small fraternity of well-led heroes first found and exploited the smallest of tears in the hegemony around them, and forged ahead by means of outrageous technical ability, wisdom beyond their years, and at times sheer force of will. In Portugal, these players, the *Geração de Ouro*, revolutionised the sport, and yet even now the fullest measure of reward for their efforts has not been fully attained. Because of them, Portuguese football is bursting at the seams with potential which would not ever have existed before the golden generation established the necessary conditions.

Forging the path

When people speak about the golden generation in Portugal, the discussion inevitably orbits around Luís Figo, often the only member of this class remembered by international football enthusiasts. While the 2000 Ballon d'Or winner's role in transforming the landscape of Portuguese football should not be understated, the term *golden generation* most commonly describes the key group of Portugal U20 players who won back-to-back World Youth Championships in 1989 and 1991.

This exceptional cadre unveiled the inimitable quality of Portuguese football to the outside world, a complicated endeavour in the time before social media, satellite television and super agents. In those days, international audiences only ever witnessed influential figures from nations such as Portugal during global tournaments. As late as the mid-90s, only an elite few, such as Atlético Madrid's Paulo Futre, had gained notoriety abroad. Until 1995, not a single Portuguese player had ever suited up for an English Premier League side. Portugal's effervescent interpretation of the game was almost entirely shrouded in mystery.

Of the small list of players who first made their way to England in the late 1990s, four were members of one or both of those fabled U20 squads who emerged victorious at the 1989 and 1991 World Youth Championships. Some, like João Pinto, had extraordinary careers in the Portuguese domestic league. Still others, such as Rui Costa, Paulo Sousa, and Fernando Couto, left enduring impressions of their own in other leagues across Europe.

During the 2019/20 season, there were 18 Portuguese players in England's top flight. Cristiano Ronaldo – a monolith in Portuguese footballing lore and one of the greatest to ever play the game – dominates Italy's Serie A. France's Ligue 1 is spattered with Portuguese talent. LaLiga is home for the 2019 Golden Boy winner, João Félix – who secured the distinction three years after Renato Sanches became the first Portuguese to ever be hailed as such in 2016.

All this from a nation of just 11 million people. All of this impossible and unimaginable before the golden generation chiselled a footpath for Portuguese football to transform the European game.

Queiroz: youth football mastermind

Prior to the 1989 World Youth Championships, Portugal's youth national teams had only ever qualified for one tournament – in 1979. For Portuguese players, the professional ceiling was to sign for one of Portugal's top three sides – Benfica, Sporting or Porto. There was no market or interest in Portuguese talent. Even the great Eusébio, who scored nine goals at the 1966 World Cup, had only left Portugal as part of a global footballing tour in the twilight of his career.

Enter Carlos Queiroz, one of the earliest in the ever-expanding catalogue of Portuguese managers and architect of the golden generation's tactical assembly.

While Queiroz would eventually spread his influence elsewhere, most recently with Iran and Colombia's national teams, he exercised two indispensable functions which – in their own time and in their own way – dissolved sporting barriers for Portuguese footballers. First, he hewed diamonds of radiant quality from the amorphous heap of Portuguese talent which unexpectedly emerged in the late 1980s. Years later, he personally guided Cristiano Ronaldo during his time at Manchester United.

In hindsight, some insist the quality of talent available to Queiroz virtually guaranteed his successes in 1989 and 1991. But in Portugal, Queiroz's methods were very progressive, especially his determination to combine a player's technical attributes with coherent discipline in order to win even the toughest football matches. A comparable approach would later be used by Fernando Santos during the senior side's unexpected *coup d'état* at Euro 2016 when they overthrew incumbent heavyweight France in extra time, the landmark achievement in Portuguese football history to date.

While Queiroz's moulding of the golden generation and work with Portuguese youth development inspired an unstoppable chain of events, it did not immediately impact Portugal's senior side. Queiroz subsequently led the *Seleção* during qualification for the 1992 European Championship and failed. The flickering of promise shown at Euro 1996 was sandwiched between more qualification failures for the World Cups of 1994 and 1998. In each of those campaigns, many of the very same players under Carlos Queiroz's guidance in 1989 and 1991 critically failed to unite their technical brilliance with defensive solidarity.

Queiroz started Portugal's engine, but the odyssey toward football prestige at senior level began poorly for the golden generation during the mid to late 90s. Even so, Queiroz's masterful approach influenced the Federation of Portuguese football. Club restructuring soon followed and the calibre of Portuguese talent soared. By the end of the 1990s, prodigiously gifted players would advance through Portugal's youth teams and into the *Seleção*.

In pursuit of destiny

The new millennium arrived. By then, the secret regarding Portuguese talent had begun to percolate out into the rest of Europe despite the national team failures of the previous decade. Key figures from those 1989 and 1991 U20 squads – Figo, Paulo Sousa, Abel Xavier, Fernando Couto and Rui Costa – were making waves outside Portugal.

The years of underachievement in the 1990s had nearly relegated them to the category of false hope, but Euro 2000 arguably became the grandest stage for Portugal's golden generation. Many in Portugal still regard this *Seleção* squad as the finest ever assembled. Here the world again witnessed the compelling symphony of attacking invention and technical artistry which characterised this transcendent group of players. The tournament was also their first genuine senior-side test against established world powers with England and Germany drawn alongside Portugal in Group A. Portugal defeated them both as well as Gheorghe Hagi's Romania, effortlessly swept aside Turkey in the quarter-final and advanced into the semi-finals against Zinedine Zidane's France, who were two years removed from winning that nation's first-ever World Cup.

The ensuing match has been considered by many to be when this group of players finally captured the essence of the *Geração de Ouro*. Though Zidane sealed Portugal's fate with a penalty in extra time, the compelling semi-final encounter with France is usually in the conversation regarding best-ever matches in European Championship history, and it established Portugal as a latent superpower, no longer a minnow.

Since 2000, the Portuguese national team has never failed to reach the finals of a major tournament, advancing to at least the semi-final four times, winning Euro 2016, and claiming the inaugural UEFA Nations League title in the summer of 2019. Nuno Gomes, who scored four goals at Euro 2000, said that 'from 2000 onwards, foreign clubs always kept their eyes open for Portuguese players'. The golden generation brought Portuguese football to life.

But their individual and collective influence on European football was far from over.

The world beckons

Jorge Mendes – perhaps the original super-agent – made his first deal in 1996 involving then-goalkeeper and current manager Nuno Espírito Santo. After Euro 2000, interest in Portuguese players exploded and Mendes was keen to exploit that fascination. Two years after Euro 2000, Jorge Mendes completed a landmark deal when he moved Hugo Viana to Newcastle for a then-record sum. Few remember Viana, but Jorge Mendes continued to invest heavily in the Portuguese youth system which proliferated in the wake of the golden generation.

Sporting Clube de Portugal's Alcochete Academy, who had already produced Luís Figo, began to cultivate extravagantly skilful players who Mendes effectively advertised to Europe's club heavyweights, a practice which continues to the present day. Portugal's domestic league progressively gained a reputation as an incubator of world-class talent. Even many foreign players would benefit from the strides made during this time period with Ángel Di María, James Rodríguez, Radamel Falcao and many others being groomed for club success across Europe. Jorge Mendes thus spread the fruit of the golden generation's labour far and wide, transforming club fortunes and even planting the seeds for Portuguese managers to build their reputations abroad.

All of this was catalysed by a less celebrated golden generation member and, indubitably, José Mourinho.

The special one and beyond

Though Portugal's national team prestige had increased remarkably after Euro 2000, more time and more brilliance from golden generation players was required to elevate Portugal's domestic league stature. Aside from Benfica's European Cup triumphs in the 1960s, FC Porto was the only Portuguese club to ever win a continental title in Europe – in 1987 when Paulo Futre's brilliance dispatched Bayern Munich.

Then Jorge Costa assumed the role of captain for José Mourinho's Porto in summer 2002.

Costa had partnered Fernando Couto, another golden generation veteran, in central defence at Euro 2000, and had earned a loan move to English Premier League side Charlton Athletic for the 2001/02 season. But Costa leapt at the opportunity to return to Porto and play under José Mourinho, who had arrived from União de Leiria in January 2002.

The temperament of the squad Mourinho wanted, which was channelled through Costa and Porto, was extraordinary, winning a treble in 2002/03 and more critically the UEFA Champions League in 2003/04. This achievement launched Mourinho's career outside Portugal with the help of the aforementioned Jorge Mendes, and Europe now began to see Portugal as a hotbed for young managerial talent as well.

Over the next 15 years, André Villas-Boas, Carlos Carvalhal, Leonardo Jardim, Marco Silva, Jorge Jesus, Pedro Martins, Fernando Santos, José Gomes, Paulo Fonseca, Nuno Espírito Santo and others entered the managerial circuit with varying degrees of success. Jorge Costa himself became a manager as did fellow golden generation member Paulo Sousa, who has enjoyed ventures in the French top flight.

The paradox

If Euro 2000 was the golden generation's coming of age party, then Euro 2004 was its chance for redemption. This was the final opportunity for the legends of the 1989 and 1991 U20 squads to deliver the senior trophy its supporters craved.

Hosted in Portugal, the *Seleção* were drawn into a difficult group and beaten in their opening match by Greece. But in each of the following matches, heroics from Figo and celestial intervention from Rui Costa launched Portugal beyond Russia, Spain, England and the Netherlands to reach the final – an unlikely rematch against Greece they would surely win this time.

But calamity struck. Angelos Charisteas scored the match's only goal and ended the dream held by Portuguese supporters all over the world – that this generation would fulfil the promise shown in 1989 and 1991.

The paradox of the golden generation was that aside from the youth championships which launched their careers, they never fully harnessed the lesson instilled by Carlos Queiroz: to equally unite skill and discipline and win the toughest matches. But the gift they gave the world and especially Portuguese football was of a far greater value. Reminiscent of the greatest tragedies in theatre, the protagonists paid the ultimate sacrifice, but in doing so a radiant hope was born and passed down to the generations that followed. Every Portuguese football accomplishment is built upon their work.

The golden generation raised the benchmark for Portuguese players. Couto was the first to earn 100 international caps for Portugal. Figo became Portugal's most-capped player of all time until Ronaldo overtook him. He also finished his career with the most assists of all time in LaLiga before being surpassed by Ronaldo, Messi, and Xavi. Abel Xavier became one of the first Portuguese globetrotters since Eusébio, a trend common among Portuguese footballers today. Rui Costa and João Pinto still reside in Portugal's top-ten list of most goals scored.

Figo, the pre-eminent member of Portugal's golden generation, came out of retirement to compete in the 2006 World Cup. He registered three assists as Portugal finished fourth. How melancholic that he would not be the one to finally lead Portugal to national team glory, but so beautiful his career lit the way for Cristiano Ronaldo. At Manchester United, Carlos Queiroz came full circle and finished his task of mentoring Portugal's golden youth by helping refine Cristiano's burgeoning career. Nearly a decade later, Ronaldo completed the unfinished work of Portugal's greatest-ever generation of players in leading the *Seleção* to European Championship glory in France.

Football is what author Simon Sinek describes as an infinite game. Players come and go. Championships are won and lost. But the game goes on and on. The golden generation contributed most toward the timeless cause of advancing Portuguese football though they never achieved the temporal measurement of football success: a trophy.

References:
KUNDERT, T., MOTZ, N. AND CURTIS S. *The Thirteenth Chapter.* Chiado Books, 2018
SINEK, S. *The Infinite Game.* Penguin, 2019.

TUGAL'S LINKS WITH AFRICA: THE PAST, PRESENT AND FUTURE

by Karan Tejwani *(@karan_tejwani26)*

IN THE 1960s, Benfica reached five European Cup finals, winning the first two and losing the next three. In 1961 and 1962, they overcame the Spanish challenge from Barcelona and Real Madrid respectively, ending their Iberian neighbours' dominance over the competition and bringing the famous trophy to Portugal for the first time. In the next three finals, the eagles of Lisbon fell to the Milanese duo of Milan and Inter before their last attempt in that decade was a loss at Wembley to Manchester United. While this was an excellent era for the club, a key trend that linked the players and these historic achievements was backgrounds, highlighting the success of immigration, integration of foreign talent and opening new doors for emerging footballers abroad.

In Benfica's successful team that started the finals in 1961 and 1962, there were four players of African descent, while that number continued in the lost final of 1963. In 1965 and 1968, there were three and two respectively. This was part of a revolution that saw African players migrate to Europe, many of whom came to Portugal, and found their feet in a country that they could relate to well. Many of the players that started those finals were from PALOP countries – *Países Africanos de Língua Oficial Portuguesa* – or Portuguese-speaking African countries, namely Angola, Cape Verde, Guinea-Bissau and Mozambique. José Águas, the star forward and captain of the team, was born in Angola while Mário Coluna, one of the world's finest midfield players at the time, was born in Mozambique.

Those two were superstars in the Portuguese capital for years and were joined by goalkeeper Costa Pereira and Joaquim Santana in the team in 1961. Eusébio, the greatest footballer in Benfica history, started in the final a year later and set the benchmark for foreign imports. Béla Guttmann, the Hungarian who managed the two successes, was a massive supporter of African imports in his team. He was also keen on expanding his club's links to the continent – specifically the four Portuguese-speaking countries – and his desire to increase and improve this unique relationship was evident in the squads while he was at the club and after he left in 1962.

Football was a favourite of these Portuguese colonies and the locals embraced the game widely. It was introduced to the people like everything else in most colonies around the world: by the colonisers through soldiers, settlers and everyone who crossed the borders to be there. Major cities across Angola and Mozambique took a quick liking to it, and it was adored by children in schools.

The sport played a major role in Portugal's campaign of cultural imperialism – something they used to impose on colonised nations. Football was introduced to these African nations in the late 19th century, and by the start of the next century, the immense popularity of football meant that small competitions in capital cities like Lourenço Marques (now Maputo, Mozambique) and Luanda (Angola) were formed.

Migration of African talent to Portugal started towards the end of the colonial era as the country's big three – Porto, Benfica and Sporting – established links and scouting networks in the African nations colonised by Portugal. African footballers had several benefits: they were passionate about the game, highly skilled and, most importantly, cheap for clubs to afford. Sebastião Lucas da Fonseca, more commonly known as Matateu, was the first example of the talent brewing in Africa. The son of a typographer, he grew up playing with a football usually made out of rags before going on to represent Mozambican clubs like João Albasinia and 1º de Maio. It was at another local team, Manjacaze, that he was noticed by João Belo, a former Belenenses player and taken across the sea to the Iberian nation. Chased by rivals FC Porto as well, he ended up signing for the club Belo was associated with.

Joining the club in 1951, Matateu's first season saw him net 17 goals, before following that up with a great 29 in the next campaign. The forward was the finest in Portugal, and at his peak during the mid-1950s, he would score goals at an alarming rate. Despite that, Matateu's trophy haul was strangely small, with just one major honour: the Portuguese Cup in 1960. Nevertheless, his greatness opened several pathways in Portugal for African players, and he goes down in history as one of the country's finest and Belenenses's reply to Eusébio, for his record of 217 goals in 278 appearances has etched his name in history. He also represented Portugal 27 times, continuing his fine scoring run by netting 13 goals for the country.

The fact that he played for Portugal came as a result of the *Estatuto do Indígena* – the Statute of the Indigenous, introduced by the country's former dictator, António Salazar. The rule gave an assimilated status to 'Europeanised' Africans, thus giving them the chance to represent the national team. Until the introduction of the rule, first in 1926 and then more formally in 1954, African immigrants essentially had no civil or legal rights, nor did they have citizenship. This was taken full advantage of in football and even after reforms introduced in 1961, it proved to be beneficial to the Portuguese national team. Matateu was the first example, then came Eusébio, without whom Portugal would not have enjoyed success at the 1966 World Cup. To this day, players of African descent such as William Carvalho and João Mário represent the country in major tournaments.

It's worth noting how the national team was severely underperforming prior to the influx and integration of African talent to their team. Between 1949 and 1955, Portugal had won just three international matches out of 20 over the six-year period, hadn't qualified for the Olympics in over two decades and were not good enough to make it to the World Cup. A dry, winless run returned once again at the end of the 1950s and it was in this period that the governing bodies started to make best use of the foreign talent they had – not just for domestic clubs, but for international matches as well. It's no coincidence that it was in the following decade that international prominence started to grow, and it was evident in England in 1966.

For several reasons, African migrants easily find their feet in Portugal and Portuguese football. The lack of linguistic and cultural barriers, as well as living in a country where they would find people with similar stories to them makes this an easier location to settle in than other countries in Europe. Additionally, Portugal provides the best pathway – especially to the countries that they formerly colonised – and has done so historically as well. The better facilities, the opportunity to make more money and an improved lifestyle all made the migration of African talent to Portugal all the more desirable. In Africa, only the North African clubs or a few in South Africa could compete with the wages and benefits provided to the players. When colonised, countries did their best to find the finest local talent, work with them and then sell them on to Portuguese clubs for financial profit.

Portugal has a vast footballing history with Mozambique – both before and after independence. After the rise to superstardom of Eusébio, they strengthened their relations with the East African nation through tours from several clubs and radio broadcasts of Portuguese domestic matches to keep the interest high and, as more Mozambican migrants became prominent in Portugal, the acceptance grew. The country's three biggest clubs, Benfica, Porto and Sporting were the subject of adoration and Mozambican clubs were named after them with their kits even bearing identical colours. Even after independence the success stories in Portugal prompted more youngsters to make their way to their nation. That all changed temporarily, however, when after independence, there was a greater desire by the local government to see their best talent remain in the country and help them grow.

In 1975, after becoming an independent nation, the Liberation Front of Mozambique, the communist party that controlled the country, adopted strategies to help the game grow and prevent Portugal from poaching their footballers. Local teams were asked to adopt a more Mozambican name and drop any hints of their

Portuguese heritage from their identities. Additionally, Portuguese clubs were banned from visiting the country for tours as the party aimed at disallowing clubs from getting a look at and subsequently snapping up players. Most damningly, however, there was a total ban on players migrating and playing abroad. This temporarily ended the relationship between the two countries and was a big blow for the European nation.

However, this regulation didn't work out well, partly due to the country's own shortcomings and partly due to older changes made by the Confederation of African Football (CAF), the governing body of football in Africa. In 1965, CAF introduced a rule that prevented a nation from fielding more than two overseas-based players in a bid to reduce player exodus. This backfired massively as players were undeterred in their wishes to play in Europe and, in 1982, the rule was removed. In Mozambique, players moved to other Africa nations such as South Africa and the ban made their national team weaker, thus forcing the government to rescind it as well in 1987. In the country itself, socio-economic conditions, a bloody civil war, immense corruption at an institutional level and bad infrastructure further ruined young footballers' prospects, meaning that the league was weaker than ever before.

The fall of the communist government at the end of the war in 1992 meant that footballing borders were opened once again and the strong relationships between Portugal and Mozambique in a football context were restored. The hunt for talent resumed and local clubs returned to their original names and links grew once again. In a survey conducted in Maputo, the Mozambican capital, in 1995, it was revealed that only 15 per cent of the local population preferred Mozambican football over Portuguese football – an identification of the impact colonisation and migration had over the country.

However, for all the positives these footballers and their migration brought over the years, some of the negatives were shocking. Racism was a vast issue at the time, and it even affected Eusébio. Wages significantly differed between white 'natural' Portuguese players and African migrants. Eusébio's transfer to Benfica in 1961 saw him become Africa's most expensive player, but he was the club's least expensive player at the time, and it took him a decade and a tough contract argument to become the club's highest-paid player. It's worth remembering that between 1961 and 1969, he had become the world's best player, spearheaded Portugal's charge at the World Cup, and won the European Cup as well as the Ballon d'Or.

Former Sporting player António Joaquim Dinis, who hailed from Angola, described the situation: 'The majority of the Angolan players who emigrated to Portugal never felt a sense of satisfaction. Not because they lacked the public's acceptance, but because of the attitudes and actions of the patrons of Portuguese football. Angolans and Mozambicans have continually suffered shameful exploitation on the part of the "big clubs". I signed a very inexpensive contract with Sporting. I won the national championship and the Portuguese Cup; I am a member of the Portuguese national team and, in spite of all this, I had wages that were inferior to the team's reserves.'

Another problem facing Eusébio was that Portugal wanted to make him exclusive to them. When other nations were striving in the 1960s – specifically Italy – dictator Salazar declared the player as a 'national treasure', which denied him the chance to move abroad. It is often believed that when other African players were linked with foreign clubs, they were surveilled by the country's security agency, while clubs mostly demanded unreal fees from suitors to shun their interest. Given that these players were in better conditions than they would be in their home countries, they had their hands tied. Not every player may have faced the same racism issues as Dinis, nor may they have been declared 'national treasures', but those who did were seriously mistreated by a complicated regime.

The relationship between Africa and Portugal in football has continued regardless. In the 21st century, there has been a huge array of African talent, or players of African descent representing the nation at major tournaments. This time around, there were more players from other PALOP countries like Cape Verde and São Tomé and Príncipe. In the side that reached the World Cup semi-final in 2006 they boasted players like Luís Boa Morte and Costinha, while the team that won Euro

2016 in France featured Nani, Renato Sanches (voted Best Young Player of the Tournament), Eliseu, William Carvalho, Danilo, João Mário and the hero of the final, Eder, who was born in Guinea-Bissau.

With the fall of the empire and the removal of the dictator, things have slightly improved for players as well. They're free to move abroad, get paid better and are held in higher regard than five decades ago. In a study from 2015, Portugal ranked second (behind Sweden) on the Migrant Integration Policy Index's ranking of nations with the best policies towards immigrants, which is encouraging. Although they don't have an official record of how many immigrants they have, it is believed to be between 200,000 and 500,000. There will certainly be more examples like Eusébio, Matateu and Coluna in the future.

BRAGA AND THE
BREAKING OF THE
BIG THREE

by Alex Goncalves *(@aljeeves)*

PORTUGUESE FOOTBALL, since what feels like the dawn of time, has been dominated almost exclusively by just three teams in the domestic game. Benfica, Porto, Sporting. *Os Três Grandes*, as they are widely referred to in the nation – 'the Big Three' in English. In the history of Portuguese football, 85 league seasons have been played, dating back to 1934. Of those, a combined 83 have been won by this magnificent trio, a startling statistic which goes to show not only the sheer scale of dominance of the three top sides in the country – a historic supremacy unrivalled amongst all the top leagues on the continent – but, with it, also the immense uphill struggle everyone else in Portugal has to close the gap. This is, of course, even more difficult in the modern game, with monetary discrepancies between the top outfits and the chasing pack growing larger and larger as the elite sides continue to generate revenue worlds apart from the average Portuguese top-flight club.

The other two emblems that can lay claim to an extraordinary title triumph are Belenenses (way back in the 1945/46 season), and Boavista, who lifted the biggest prize in Portuguese football as recently as 2001. Boavista are perhaps the best model from recent history that illustrates that it is possible for a club to break up the established hierarchy of the Portuguese game and topple the Big Three. But it is incredibly difficult; the need to finish above not just one of the historic trio, but all three simultaneously, is a beyond daunting task, particularly sustaining that challenge on the established clubs year on year. Boavista's ability to crack into the top three consistently lasted just four seasons, finishing second, fourth, first and second between 1998 and 2002. In the 22 campaigns prior to that, they only finished in the top 3 twice – while they haven't even finished in the top five of the Primeira Liga since 2002, either. Matters away from the field completely disrupted their ability to maintain their place as a genuinely competitive team in Portuguese football, but their spell at the very top end of the league table as genuine title rivals was a beacon of hope for many clubs, a stint forever etched into the history of the Portuguese top flight.

Braga, however, are moving mountains to be the latest club to mount a serious challenge on the existing establishment – and though they, unlike Boavista, have never won the league title, early signs suggest that they may be as well placed, if not better placed, to disrupt the Big Three over a prolonged period of time. Braga's remarkable consistency has already bettered that of Boavista, as seen by their dominance against the rest of the pack in Portuguese football. Prior to the COVID-19-affected 2019/20 season, Braga finished in the top four 11 times in the previous 16 league campaigns; by contrast, in the 16 campaigns leading up to and including Boavista's most recent finish in the top four of the Primeira Liga (their second-place finish in 2002), Boavista secured just ten top-four finishes.

Braga, therefore, are set to better Boavista's top-four record over 16 seasons – and, unlike their counterparts, there is absolutely no sign that they are set to fall down the standings – and divisions – in the dramatic manner in which Boavista did. That is because not only have Braga been grappling with the Big Three in the domestic game for a sustained period of time already, but their long-term future looks highly promising, with a talented squad and plenty of prospects coming through to match the ambitions of the club president and fans. They are, with the right management, ready to challenge the Big Three in Portuguese football for the foreseeable future and can even begin dreaming about mounting a serious title challenge. They are changing the very nature of Portuguese football – and the Big Three is in the process of irreversibly being altered to forge a new, more competitive 'Big Four'. And that can only be a good thing for Portuguese football.

To illustrate Braga's rise to becoming a domestic force to be reckoned with, there is no better place to begin than at the start of the decade. It was then, in the 2009/10 season, that Braga made history by causing a major upset. It was the year that *Os Guerreiros* finally fully disrupted the shared dynasty of the Big Three in Portuguese football, finishing second – their standalone highest-ever finish in the top flight. While they fell short of lifting the biggest prize that Portuguese football has to offer – finishing just five points behind Benfica in the league standings on 71 points – Braga proved their ability to directly compete with the best Portugal have to offer, fully upsetting the apple cart by finishing above not one, but two of the established Big Three.

That in itself is a remarkable achievement – but it becomes even more sensational when you look at the sheer gulf between them and Sporting during that campaign as they finished an astonishing 23 points ahead of the Lisbon club, the Lions languishing in fourth on just 48 points after all 30 league games had been played.

But bragging rights weren't all that Braga earned for that magnificent season, as their second-place finish in the league ultimately earned them the prestigious honour of being one of Portugal's two UEFA Champions League representatives for the 2010/11 season. The repercussions of their achievement were therefore major, and ensured their extraordinary league campaign not only reverberated around the nation, but across the continent too, with Braga undoubtedly one of the few highly surprising inclusions in Europe's most illustrious club tournament that year, marking the first time in their entire history that they qualified for the UEFA Champions League, entering the competition at the third qualifying round.

The *Arsenalistas* managed to continue to surprise the continent though, managing to get through both rounds of qualification to reach the group stage of Europe's primary club competition, beating Celtic in the third qualifying round before knocking out LaLiga giants Sevilla in the play-off, beating the Spanish outfit 1-0 at home and 3-4 away to advance to the competition proper. Their valiant Champions League campaign came to an end at the group stage, though, as they finished on a highly respectable nine points, behind Shakhtar Donetsk and Arsenal. However, they did still achieve a third-place finish in the group, meaning their European adventure continued into the Europa League.

And it was there that Braga truly changed people's opinions of the unheralded Minho club as they pulled off some stunning results, beating each of Lech Poznań, Liverpool and Dynamo Kyiv over two legs to advance to the Europa League semi-final, where they were drawn against Benfica. Few would have fancied Domingos Paciência's side to hbe able to defeat their compatriots over two legs but, against all odds, Braga caused a major upset, knocking out the reigning Portuguese champions on away goals and advancing to the final of a major continental competition to round off a stunning couple of campaigns. Facing Porto in a surreal all-Portuguese final, Braga were edged out, defeated 1-0 in Dublin as their exceptional season ended in crippling disappointment. That day remains one of the greatest in Braga's history though, and it is still one of the most impressive achievements in Europa League history to date.

Doing as well as they did in the Europa League, it would be expected that their league form would drop off. And it did, Braga picking up just 46 points across the season. They still finished fourth though, showing that even with the hefty distraction of a spectacular Europa League run, Braga maintained their place as the best of the rest nationally. That they managed to follow up their stunning showing in the 2009/10 Primeira Liga with equally exceptional Champions League and Europa League displays and a respectable domestic season indicates that they were, and are, more than a one-season wonder. And they have shown as much since, their streak of challenging the three elite teams in the country unwavering, the sole exception coming in 2013/14.

Their League Cup Final victory over Porto in 2013, for example, was a huge moment in the club's history, while their Portuguese Cup triumph just three years later took things one step further, winning the biggest cup competition in the country for the first time since 1966, again defeating Porto in the final. What followed was their truly extraordinary 2017/18 Primeira Liga campaign where they earned a tally of 75 points; it may have somehow only earned Abel Ferreira's men a fourth-place finish in the Portuguese top flight, but it was the highest points total ever obtained by Braga in a single season as they finished 24 points above fifth-placed Rio Ave. A gulf that size is truly remarkable, and the fact that Braga were so much closer to first place than their nearest competitor is testament to the progress the club have been making year on year.

And if that was insufficient to illustrate Braga's truly extraordinary exploits, not only did they go on to make the top four in the league standings alongside Benfica, Porto and Sporting in the following campaign as well, but they were also the same four outfits that made up the semi-finals of both the Portuguese League Cup and Portuguese Cup too. It marked the first – and, to date, only – time since the League Cup was introduced in 2007 that the same four teams completely dominated all three domestic competitions by both occupying the four top spots in the Primeira Liga standings and reaching the final four of Portugal's two domestic cup tournaments all in the same campaign. There may be no better indication of Braga's ascension to the highest echelon of the national game than that.

That said, as tremendous as Braga were during Abel Ferreira's reign at the club, it could be argued that it is actually the recent 2019/20 season which illustrates better than any other Braga's ability to compete with the top sides in the land. Although the start of the domestic campaign was unconvincing, with Braga sitting eighth in the table in mid-December with just 18 points after 14 games, their Europa League campaign was exceptional, qualifying for the group stage after beating Brøndby and Spartak Moscow in the qualifying rounds before shocking the continent by topping their highly challenging group, containing a resurgent Wolverhampton Wanderers, Turkish giants Beşiktaş and reigning Slovakian champions Slovan Bratislava, in exhilarating style. Though their league form was faltering, with the side's points tally far below expectations, their European campaign indicated that they were better than their league form suggested, and it was only a matter of time before they witnessed an upsurge in their performance levels.

Indeed, in a highly surprising – and in many people's eyes, an undeserved – move to sack head coach Ricardo Sá Pinto, Braga turned to inexperienced Rúben Amorim as manager, and the form under the then 34-year-old was bordering on the extraordinary as Braga thumped Belenenses 7-1 away from home in his first match in charge, and followed that up with nine wins in their next ten matches across all competitions, including five wins in five against the Big Three of Benfica, Porto and Sporting. A truly extraordinary achievement, and surely unmatched in the history of Portuguese football. Not only going unbeaten against the three most illustrious sides in the country in five consecutive matches against them but beating them on each of those occasions. Not only that, but with one of those victories versus Sporting coming in the League Cup semi-final and another against Porto in the final, Amorim led Braga to cup glory just 34 days into his tenure. Not many managers in world football can lay claim to that.

Braga did go on to crash out of the Europa League against Rangers, and the managerial revelation Rúben Amorim has since been snapped up by Sporting CP, but between Amorim's first match at the helm of the club and the unprecedented moment the league was suspended in March 2020 due to the escalation of the COVID-19 outbreak, Braga were undisputedly the best team in all of Portugal – and that sets a highly encouraging tone in their bid to fulfil their lofty ambitions. Will they ever win the Primeira Liga? It's impossible to answer with absolute certainty, but you can say with a good deal of confidence that Braga's days at the top end of the Portuguese game are far from over. Dead is the traditional Big Three and born is the advent of the Big Four.

THE GENIUS OF BOBBY ROBSON IN PORTUGAL

by Joe Brennan *(@j4brennan)*

'There is not a person I would put one inch over Bobby Robson.' José Mourinho, 2019.

'If we score a goal, it's fine, it's great, but let's try for another. And if we get another, excellent, but the game continues, and we will look for yet another goal. We have to keep attacking and attacking, to get as many goals as we can.'
Bobby Robson, somewhere over Europe, 1992.

HIGH UP in the skies over a cloudy continent, the stormy atmosphere that rocked the plane from side to side was replicated by the passengers' emotions on board. The deflated, defeated Sporting CP squad were travelling by air for the last time and would no longer be required to make any more foreign trips for the rest of the season. While the majority of staff were more than disheartened, resigned to their seats having failed to complete their European objective, one man was restless and unable to contain the volts of angry energy that ran through his body. 'It was spectacular,' recalls Robson in his autobiography, 'President Sousa Cintra grabbed the microphone from the plane's intercom and announced to everyone that the coach would be [sacked] the next day.'

Goals from Leo Lainer, Adi Hütter and Martin Amerhauser had turned around a 0-2 away defeat and put Casino Salzburg into the UEFA Cup quarter-finals and now Robson was an ex-manager. As Sousa had shouted the message to the players, staff and journalists in Portuguese, Robson's personal translator who sat by his side – a bilingual schoolteacher called José Mourinho – whispered the message in English and Robson learned of his fate.

A successful spell at PSV Eindhoven had led Sousa Cintra – never a man of tranquillity and reason – to hire Robson as Sporting Clube de Portugal's manager in 1992. Just two years prior to arriving in Portugal, Robson had led England to the World Cup semi-finals on Italian soil, cruelly losing to West Germany on penalties. Now though, he was unemployed. But he would have to hear it again, only this time not from a height of 30,000 feet.

The following day, Mourinho was called into the club offices to repeat the message he had whispered on the plane; and Robson found himself again on the wrong side of one of Cintra's infamous explosions.

'[Robson] didn't want to believe it,' reported *Mais Football*, shortly after the news had been leaked; his team had just lost 3-0 away at Casino Salzburg (now FC Red Bull Salzburg) but it was by no means the end of the season for Sporting CP. For the first time in 15 years, the *Leões* were top of the first division and on course to win the title. Robson left the offices in his car, silently but with a polite smile of genuine appreciation, courteously stopping to shake hands with fans who understood well the broken situation that rotted away at the heart of Portuguese football.

The man from Durham had, in a very short time, managed to create a Sporting team that had reacted well to his casual, *laissez faire* managerial style: players such as Luis Figo and Stan Valckx had propelled Sporting CP to the top in an incredibly short time. The personality of Robson and his natural ability to gain respect and trust in his methods was key to his management style. Carlos Queiroz was immediately hired by Cintra, leading some people to believe the deal had been done behind Robson's back. Ever gracious in victory and defeat, the manager turned his back on Sporting CP and walked away.

Estádio das Antas, Porto, Portugal. 1994.

For a brief second, Robson forgets there is somebody transcribing the interview he is giving at his Porto unveiling: his County Durham accent returns, along with his quick-fire word speed; his body language shifts

– he is now beating his heart with an open hand – and a huge grin has appeared from nowhere. 'Very special. Those games [against Sporting CP] are the sort of games I like. Those games are the sort of games I cannot give up.' Then he remembers that he is a professional manager and is probably, for the benefit of the poor translator, required to slow down: 'Sporting CP will be a special game; I obviously want to beat them because Futebol Clube de Porto is my life now.'

The call came within a month. Jorge Nuno Pinto da Costa, the longest-serving club president in world football, interpreted the whimsical decision by Cintra as an opportunity. Porto, like Sporting prior to Robson's arrival, had been in a slump: attendances had dwindled to under 10,000. Robson quickly set up camp: his translator Mourinho – who was now promoted to assistant coach – had agreed to travel with him north from Lisbon to Porto. The club's Observational Department gained a new member too: a 16-year-old Porto fan called André Villas-Boas lived in the same apartment block as Robson and had been leaving detailed scouting reports in his letterbox every Friday.

Upon meeting in the courtyard of the building, the young man astounded Robson not only with his fluent English, but his in-depth knowledge of football, somewhat gleaned from his fascination with the computer game, *Championship Manager*. Robson, as open-minded as ever, took a leap of faith and asked the club to pay for his coaching licence course in Scotland

and then sent him to his former club, Ipswich Town, in an effort to get the youngster as many in-action minutes as possible on the sidelines.

Robson's first match in charge was a 0-2 win against SC Salgueiros in the *Taça de Portugal*, followed by a 2-0 loss against league leaders Benfica. Porto would then go on something of a free-scoring run: 18-0 was the aggregate score over his next four games as they demolished Marítimo, CD Aves, FC Famalicão and SC Braga.

Their next match was a disappointing single-goal loss against Anderlecht in the Champions League, which was quickly reverted in the return leg, with Secretário and Drulović on the scoresheet. After that, Porto would not lose another game in Portugal – Stoichkov and Koeman would knock them out of the European Cup semi-final against Cruyff's Barcelona – but the once-disillusioned Porto faithful were enamoured by Robson's grit and passion: emotions that he projected on to the players, who were clearly playing for their manager and the joy of winning. Porto finished runners-up in Robson's first half-season, but the real glory came in the domestic cup competition. Defeating relegated Amadora in the semi-finals led to a final against, of all the teams in Portugal, Robson's ex-employers: Sporting CP. In his first interview, he had remarked how the games against Sporting CP would be special. Now he had a chance to show them – and Sousa Cintra – that they had made a mistake in letting him go.

Taça de Portugal, Final.
Estádio Nacional, Oeiras (Lisbon), Portugal.
Sunday, 5 June 1994.

Three sides of the sold-out stadium held just under 40,000 fans, all with their scarves aloft, depressingly sat behind a huge running track. The grassy hills surrounding the stadium glowed green in the hot sun as the players lined up and respected the national anthem. The opponents were an electric, attacking team, but Robson had brought new life to Porto; the stage was set.

The game was tight with occasional moments of skill, but neither team was able to create and put away a clear chance. The game finished 0-0 and a replay awaited.

Porto XI: Baia; Secretário, Pinto, Couto, Aloísio; Jorge, Santos, Andre (Filipe, 87'), Tomofte (Cuoto, 87'); Folha, Drulović

Sporting XI: Lemajić; Nélson, Valckx, Torres, Peixe (Marinho, 78'); Capucho, Sousa, Cadete, Figo; Pacheco (Poejo, 87'), Juskowiak

Five days later …

Taça de Portugal, Finalíssima.
Estádio Nacional, Oeiras (Lisbon), Portugal.
Friday, 10 June 1994.

The lack of finishing witnessed just days earlier was no more after a fine strike from Rui Jorge half an hour into the game. In such a short time, Robson had brought the Porto team back to a level where they could repeatedly compete physically and mentally with Sporting, despite an equaliser from Vujačić. The game would finish as a draw; it was in extra time that the winner was to be decided.

The whistle blew for the final 30 minutes and Porto came flying out the blocks. Paulinho Santos's header was met with fury as Sporting CP centre-back Peixe jumped and swiped the ball away with his hand. The referee did not hesitate and neither did Aloísio, who calmly slotted away the resulting penalty.

Robson held himself together; he was, as ever, courteous to the Sporting CP president and kept his celebrations curtailed to show maximum respect to his rivals. But this was a turning point. Porto had just gone toe-to-toe with a team that was far superior and managed to come out on top.

Sporting XI: Lemajić; Nélson, Vujačić (Jorge, 67'), Torres (Marinho, 65'), Peixe; Capucho, Poejo, Sousa, Cadete, Figo; Pacheco

Porto XI: Baia; Secretário, Pinto, Couto, Aloísio; Jorge, Santos, Andre (Vinha, 82'), Tomofte (Filipe 67'); Folha, Drulović

Goals: Rui Jorge, 35'; Vujačić, 55'; Aloísio, 91'

1994/95 season

The significance of the cup win against Sporting CP can never be overstated when talking about its impact. Porto's board knew the opportunistic phone call to Robson after his dismissal was a stroke of genius; the club were now firmly back in the picture and everyone – most importantly the players – believed they had what it took to achieve real success. The following season was Robson's first full term in charge in Portugal, and it was the chance for him to truly get his feet under the table and prove his worth. Incredible man-management skills that he possessed in his repertoire meant that Porto quickly sat at the top of the table. His calm, assured nature had the effect of keeping everyone in the squad happy and content with their role when their time came.

Ruthless in both attack and defence, Porto lost just a solitary game in the league, conceding just 15 goals. In the entire season they scored over three goals on 16 separate occasions and kept 32 clean sheets. Mourinho saw his role grow substantially as assistant coach in what became a formative year for the Portuguese apprentice. Robson would use him as his confidant; they would often spend hours poring over the minutiae of the game together, bouncing tactical ideas off one another. He was also tasked with preparing scouting reports that, in the words of Robson himself, were 'as good as anything I had ever seen'. The team, having had half a season and a full pre-season campaign to perfect their skills, were at their peak; under the management of the unlikely duo, they played thrilling, attacking football with an assured, confident defensive structure. Porto didn't lose a game until October, and the nickname Bobby Five-0 would quickly surface from the Portuguese media, a nod to the incredibly high-scoring home games he would oversee.

'All I had was a constantly blocked nose ... the firms who make inhalant sticks have never had a better customer.' – Bobby Robson.

1995/96 season

The year 1995 would turn out to be the one in which Robson would have to overcome his greatest challenge. After having an appointment unknowingly booked by his wife, and being too embarrassed to cancel it, Robson went to the doctors, the sole complaint being about having a blocked nose. 'Elsie, please, I haven't got time for this,' Robson complained. But doctors found a rare yet deadly form of cancer, known as a malignant melanoma, below his eye. If the doctor's words of him needing an operation 'yesterday' were indicative of the seriousness of the situation, Robson's personality came through overwhelmingly in his response: 'But I'm going back to Porto tomorrow.' Instead of boarding the plane, the 62-year-old quickly underwent surgery. An incision was made from his right eye to his mouth and the skin was peeled back like wrapping paper while doctors tunnelled through his face, removing his teeth on the way. The gap that the tumour left now held a pink rubber plug that kept his face from collapsing.

Whatever else was removed from his mouth was substituted with a prosthetic upper jaw. Typically, this did little to hold Robson back, and he was in the dugout before long; miraculously only missing the first few months of the season, in which the players would not lose a league game. Whether it was on the touchline or in the restaurant by the side of the Estádio da Antas (usually eating his favourite white scabbard fish), Robson devoted all the time and energy his body would allow to FC Porto.

Robson's return was hugely impactful for Porto, who finished the season as champions having scored 2.71 goals per game. It was the first season in Portugal that wins would be awarded three points, after the rule from FIFA was implemented, meaning Porto topped the league with 84 points from 26 games.

Robson, after having turned Barcelona down twice previously, signed for them in 1996 with a near-impossible task: to replace Johan Cruyff. Robson signed Ronaldo Nazário (after a curious recommendation from former Sporting CP player Stan Valckx) and Barça, in a single season, would go on to win a Copa del Rey, the Supercopa de España and the European Cup Winners' Cup. The targeted media criticism of his pragmatic but effective style was relentless and eventually wore him down. In spite of the trophies, Robson quickly moved on and returned to PSV a year later.

But, 1,159km west, Robson remained a hero, an eternal icon who brought the spark of sport back to

Portugal. When he arrived on the peninsula just three years previous, two of the most historical teams in the country were on their knees; football's light was going out, but no more.

Robson died on 31 July 2009 after a battle with lung cancer. The football world poured out endless tributes and homages to the man who some considered the greatest English football manager of all time. Although he arguably left Portugal too soon, the foundations he built meant Porto would go on to win the next three league titles. The tribute produced by the club after his death opens with Robson stood alongside his translator. A simple nudge in the shoulder speaks a thousand words for him to translate; Mourinho knew what to say with just a simple touch. He is now a legend at Porto and dedicates his schooling entirely to Robson: 'I owe him so much ... I got from him the idea of what it was to be a top coach.' Mourinho won six major honours with the *Dragões,* including guiding them to two league titles and becoming the best team in Europe in 2004. Bobby Robson was the embodiment of dignity and professionalism; he is one of the few people whose impact was so profound that it will live on forever, standing the test of time in the memories of the fans and in the glory of football.

Reference:
ROBSON, B. *Bobby Robson: Farewell but not Goodbye – My Autobiography,* Hodder Paperbacks, 2006

CLOSING THE CIRCLE: HOW A BEAUTIFUL SYMMETRY WILL FOREVER LINK JOSÉ MOURINHO AND ANDRÉ VILLAS-BOAS

by Jake Sandy *(@JakeSandyFC)*

TO QUOTE Ecclesiastes 1:9: 'What has been will be again, what has been done will be done again; there is nothing new under the sun.' Being a country deeply rooted in Catholicism, many Portuguese people will be familiar with this quote. Although, it must be said, there are likely far fewer that have considered how this pertains to football in their country.

On 21 May 2003, a relatively inexperienced Portuguese manager, who had never played football at an elite level, lifted the UEFA Cup to complete a historic treble in his first full season as FC Porto manager. His name? José Mourinho. Almost eight years later, 18 May 2011, the world had turned full circle as another relatively inexperienced Portuguese manager, who had never played football at an elite level, lifted the Europa League (the UEFA Cup's successor) to complete a historic treble in his first full season as Porto manager. The only difference? His name was André Villas-Boas.

Although they both publicly downplay the parallels between themselves, the two men are opposite sides of the same coin, a master and his apprentice, a teacher and his student. The inextricable link between them is far deeper than their personal association and extends back to the earliest parts of their respective careers. Tracing their paths back through a dozen clubs, hundreds of matches and tens of thousands of hours spent in football, leads to just one man – Sir Bobby Robson.

Despite his success at coaching at a relatively low level, the launch pad for Mourinho's much-storied managerial career, ironically, came from a career change as he became the translator for English manager Bobby Robson who had just been appointed manager at Sporting CP. Despite Robson being sacked after just five months in Lisbon, the pair would discuss coaching and tactics during this brief period and, suitably impressed with Mourinho's knowledge in these areas and his prowess in compiling scouting reports, Robson invited Mourinho to continue working with him at his new club – Porto. As well as the new surroundings in Portugal's second-largest city, Mourinho had also worked his way up the pecking order to become Robson's assistant manager.

As fate would have it, this move was the catalyst for the remarkable coincidences that led to Mourinho and Villas-Boas crossing paths for the first time. Born to a middle-class family living in central Porto, Villas-Boas was a typical, if slightly obsessive, football fan who followed his local club with the dedication and enthusiasm that made it the centre of his universe. Not just content with attending games though, he would frequently turn up to school in the days following a match with detailed notes on the tactical and technical aspects of Porto's performance – ready to furnish anyone who would listen with his comprehensive thoughts about the fixture. It was this readiness to engage with anyone about his favourite subject, and a healthy dose of chance, that ultimately led to the beginning of this young man's path to the top of the game.

Villas-Boas was just 16 years old when, in 1993, Robson took over managerial duties at the Porto-based club who were coming off the back of a season where they had to settle for second place in the Primeira Divisão, finishing just two points behind Sporting CP. As fate would have it, Robson and his family moved into the same apartment complex that housed the Villas-Boas family. It was the courtyard of this building where the two first met, with the young football fan seizing his opportunity to question the Englishman on why he was leaving Domingos Paciência – his favourite player – on the bench so frequently. Most managers with his level of prestige in the game would have been aghast, and possibly even furious, at the temerity of Villas-Boas to openly question their decisions. However, as many can attest to, Sir Bobby Robson was not 'most managers'. Rather than scold the young man for his impertinence, Robson chose to indulge him and, impressed by his precocious nature, encouraged him to stay in touch.

Villas-Boas made the most of this offer and would frequently slide notes under the door of Robson's apartment containing match reports and tactical analysis, even being so bold as to offer advice for upcoming fixtures. It's impossible to know whether the Porto manager ever actually heeded the recommendations of his unlikely friend; however, suitably impressed by the passion and dedication shown by the young man, Robson invited him to view the team's training sessions – a decision that led to Villas-Boas meeting José Mourinho for the first time.

Upon obtaining his UEFA C licence at the Scottish Football Association (paid for by Porto at the behest of Robson), Villas-Boas returned to Portugal and became an analyst and youth-team coach at the club that laid the foundations for his fledgling career. Working directly under Robson, he was now a colleague of Mourinho and, as such, their relationship became more of a mentor and his protégé – he evidently saw something special in his young compatriot that stuck with him for a long time.

Robson's impressive tenure at the Estádio das Antas led to Barcelona seeking to employ him as their manager ahead of the 1996/97 season to fill the void left by the departure of Johan Cruyff. After agreeing terms with the Catalan club, most notably his stipulation that they allow Mourinho to remain as his assistant, he left Portugal and Villas-Boas behind as he headed for Spain.

Villas-Boas remained in his role as analyst and youth-team coach until December 1999 when, aged just 22, he left his hometown club and travelled 4,000 miles to become the technical director of the British Virgin Islands' national team. Looking back on the somewhat brash way he first engaged with Robson and obtained his first coaching licence whilst he was still technically underage, this decision was perhaps indicative of a young man who had lofty ambitions and was confident that he was destined to realise them.

His brief stint in the Caribbean lasted just five months though as the team lost the two games they were involved in during his tenure, both against Bermuda, with an aggregate scoreline of 14-1 across the home and away fixtures.

Upon his arrival, he immediately impressed the head of the British Virgin Islands Football Association (BVIFA), Kenrick Grant, with his detailed and computerised training programmes for both the youth and senior teams. However, the optimism on Grant's side didn't last long as, in an interview with author Patrick Barclay for his book *Mourinho: Further Anatomy of a Winner*, he stated that Villas-Boas was 'very quiet', 'never really settled or focused' in his new climes, and would 'return to Portugal' whenever he had the opportunity. With this testimony in mind, it's unsurprising that Grant confessed: 'One time, he wrote to me asking for a reference and I said I was sorry but could not do that.' It appears as though this difficult job came too soon for the young coach, who went on to return to Portugal and reassume his role as a youth-team coach at Porto. It was, however, this failure that was the catalyst for the most important event in his career so far – a reunion with José Mourinho.

After a season spent as Robson's assistant in Barcelona, the latter's promotion to becoming the club's 'general manager' led to Mourinho working more closely with their new first-team manager, Louis van Gaal. This was an important moment in Mourinho's career as the Dutchman allowed him to take responsibility for coaching Barcelona B and even the first team in the Copa Catalunya.

This was a watershed moment in the Portuguese coach's career as it gave him the platform to build up his skills as a manager in his own right, something that persuaded the then Benfica president, João Vale e Azevedo, to appoint Mourinho as their manager during the first month of the 2000/01 season, replacing Jupp Heynckes. After resigning from this role after just four months, he then went on to spend six months at União de Leiria who he led to fifth position in the Primeira Liga (a club record that is yet to be surpassed). His impressive performance at Leiria led to him being offered the reins at Porto – thus allowing him to sit in the same hallowed seat as his idol.

On reflection, the reunion between Mourinho and Villas-Boas seems almost like the plot of a Hollywood film. Two men who had entirely different trajectories to the position they were in, but yet shared so many similarities in their passion and fervour for the game. Villas-Boas worked for Mourinho's technical team on a part-time basis during what remained of the 2001/02 season and it was only really the next season that both men would settle into their respective roles and achieve something magnificent.

At this point, Villas-Boas was taken on as a full-time member of the backroom staff at the club with his role being loosely defined as 'opposition scout'. Villas-Boas lived and breathed football during this period: he would travel the world to watch the games of upcoming opponents, spy on their training sessions whilst wearing disguises, and watch video upon video of their recent matches. Then, he would return to his office and spend countless hours painstakingly compiling dossiers on their opponents' tactics, writing individual reports on their entire squad, and even going so far as to make personalised DVDs for each member of the Porto team focusing on the player that they would be facing in the upcoming match.

In their book, *André Villas-Boas: Special Too*, Jaime R. Pinho and Luís Miguel Pereira include excerpts from Villas-Boas's report on Celtic, Porto's opponents in the 2003 UEFA Cup Final. It truly is a spellbinding piece of work on the Glaswegian club that breaks down every aspect of the team both in open play and at set pieces to uncover the nuances in their personnel and style. To credit this report with delivering their 3-2 victory is, of course, hyperbolic, but to say that it was not a pivotal component to the club winning their first major European trophy since the 1986/87 season is an understatement to the truly Herculean task he undertook to put it together.

Villas-Boas's role, which Mourinho later described as being his 'eyes and ears', was an essential part of the success that the pair enjoyed throughout Europe over the next few years. As well as the aforementioned UEFA Cup, that Porto team won the Primeira Liga title and the Taça de Portugal that season to claim a treble; a feat they went on to replicate the next season as they claimed another league title, won the Supertaça Cândido de Oliveira and exchanged the UEFA Cup for the more prestigious Champions League trophy.

After two full seasons in Porto, Mourinho and his backroom staff moved to Chelsea where he claimed back-to-back Premier League titles (the first with a record-breaking points total of 91), as well as adding a league cup and an FA Community Shield to their trophy cabinet. After their time in West London had come to an end, Mourinho, still with Villas-Boas in tow, then travelled to Italy to take over the reins at Inter Milan, who had recently sacked Roberto Mancini ahead of the 2008/09 season. This proved to be the final chapter in the tale of their working relationship as tensions between the pair began to rise during their time in Lombardy.

After Mourinho's dismissal from Chelsea in September 2007, Villas-Boas also found himself unemployed and chose to embark on a temporary career in the media – appearing as a football analyst on the Portuguese sports channel Sport TV (a not too surprising move given the similar role he had during the 2006 World Cup at another channel, SIC). He was an instant hit in this new venture as his tactical knowledge was far in excess of that of a typical pundit and set him apart in what was a crowded field. Despite this personal success, however, this kind of exposure began to open a rift between himself and Mourinho since, according to Pinho and Pereira, he 'never particularly appreciated his assistant's desire to play a more leading role'.

If this was the event that caused the cracks to start showing, then, in April 2008, when Villas-Boas vocalised his desire to leave Mourinho's camp to become a coach in his own right, that smashed it beyond repair. Incensed by the perceived lack of respect on the part of his assistant, Mourinho froze him out immediately. This signalled the end of their professional association that had lasted almost seven years and spanned three countries and, ultimately, left Villas-Boas still technically employed at Inter Milan, but with no job there to speak of.

Being cast aside by his mentor in such a callous manner may have seemed like the lowest of lows to the aspiring coach who was still just 31 years old. However, unperturbed by this setback, Villas-Boas then set out on his journey to go it alone and become the sole manager of a club. By the end of October 2009, he had already achieved this ambition as he found himself in the dugout at Académica de Coimbra who were residing at the bottom of the Primeira Liga.

It didn't take long for the novice manager to have an impact on his new squad and, despite his youth, he quickly established himself as a leader of men in the dressing room. With his new training regime based around the concept of 'tactical periodisation' (something Mourinho is very closely associated with) and his attention to detail when it came to team briefings ahead of games, the club quickly found their fortunes reversed. They managed to finish the season in 11th position – a miraculous recovery from a team that many were sure were bound for relegation before their new manager assumed his position.

After two approaches from Sporting CP to secure his signature throughout this season fell through, he was head-hunted by Porto to replace their coach, Jesualdo Ferreira, who they planned to dispense with at the end of the season. After agreeing personal terms with the club, his return was sealed. André Villas-Boas would be returning to his boyhood club to become the youngest-ever manager in the club's 126-year history.

In a weird twist of fate that is perhaps appropriate for this particular tale, Villas-Boas would be taking charge of Porto after just 30 games as a professional manager which was just one less than Mourinho's 31 when he took the role slightly less than eight years earlier.

Villas-Boas's first, and only, season at the club was as trophy-laden as any manager could wish for. He was aided by a squad full of players who went on to dominate European football for the next decade including goalkeeper and club captain Helton, defenders Maicon and Nicolás Otamendi, midfielders João Moutinho, Fredy Guarín and James Rodríguez, and attacking outlets like Hulk and Radamel Falcao.

This team completed an unprecedented invincible season in the Primeira Liga with a record of 27 wins and three draws, won the Supertaça Cândido de Oliveira and the Taça de Portugal, before rounding off the season with a victorious run in the Europa League. Excluding the Portuguese Super Cup which was unavailable to Mourinho in his first full season, this exactly matched, and from a points perspective even exceeded, the achievements of his former mentor at Porto and thus the circle was complete. Two men who took radically different, yet completely intertwined, paths to becoming manager of Porto ended their first complete season with an eerie symmetry.

This historical quadruple made Villas-Boas the talk of European football with all manner of suitors looking to secure his signature ahead of the 2011/12 season.

The club that finally won this battle was, of course, Chelsea. To go back to the very next line of Ecclesiastes: 'Sometimes people say, "Here is something new!" But actually, it is old; nothing is ever truly new.'

References:
BARCLAY, P. *Mourinho: Further Anatomy of a Winner*, Orion, 2015
PEREIRA, L.M AND PINHO, J.R: *André Villas-Boas: Special Too*, Dewi Lewis Media Ltd, 2011

WHEN BOAVISTA
SHOOK PORTUGAL

by Michael Gallwey *(@michael95angelo)*

THE FINANCIAL inequality that exists within football has been placed increasingly under a microscope in recent years, with the rise of Paris Saint-Germain and Manchester City into the ranks of the super clubs due to their backing by oil-rich states. Currently, 13 of the 54 top European leagues are experiencing their longest runs of domination by single clubs, from Juventus (eight seasons), to FC Santa Coloma of Andorra (six seasons). With the scrutiny heightened after Leicester's improbable title success in 2015/16, there has been an increase in the public desire to level the playing field and give those outside of the elite a chance to catch up.

One league often overlooked in terms of a monopoly of success is the Portuguese league. Since the title rotates between three clubs, the dominance of certain clubs in Portugal is often missed. Since the league was founded back in 1934/35, only five clubs have managed to capture the title. Outside of Belenenses in 1945/46, no other team had won the Primeira Divisão other than Porto, Benfica and Sporting Lisbon prior to the 2000/01 season when Boavista upset the order of Portuguese football. However, Boavista's story was not a complete fairy tale nor did it last a single season.

Under the presidency of Valentim Loureiro, Boavista had become a consistent top-division team, maintaining regular mid-table finishes with occasional cup successes. Considering the circumstances that clubs in Portugal faced, this run was seemingly the ceiling for all outside the big three. Yet, when Valentim was replaced as president by his son, João, the younger Loureiro set about a revolution in transforming Boavista into a contender rather than an also-ran.

Having won the 1997 Taça de Portugal, Boavista started the 1997/98 season with a new president and a spot in the penultimate Cup Winners' Cup. Despite the optimism ahead of the new season, Boavista had to still live within their financial means, having to sell their key players to the bigger clubs, both domestically and abroad. Their two best players were offloaded, with Jimmy Floyd Hasselbaink moving to Leeds United and Erwin Sánchez being prised away by Benfica.

During that season, Loureiro made what would turn out to be the most pivotal personnel signing in Boavista's history: employing Portuguese international Jaime Pacheco as the manager. Pacheco, a European Cup winner with Porto in 1987, favoured a hard-working, primarily defensive approach, trying to make Boavista hard to beat and have them work harder than any other team. In his first full season in charge, Pacheco managed to guide his team into second place, the highest finish since 1975/76.

The subsequent Champions League run was crucial to Boavista's continued growth, but it ultimately proved a distraction. A small squad with added European games is always a difficult task to navigate and the big three in Portugal had seemingly relegated Boavista back into a 'best of the rest' team, with a fourth-place finish in 1999/2000 representing what was perceived to be the ceiling for the team. Little did everyone know what was building in the smaller club from Porto.

Prior to the 2000/01 season, everything seemed in place for Boavista to continue their run as the best team outside of the big three with little more expected. The squad had been largely kept the same, made up of young hopefuls, journeymen and those with a point to prove having been released from the top Portuguese teams. One such player was former Boavista star Sánchez.

One of Bolivia's greatest players, Sánchez had become a legend at Boavista during the 1990s, excelling so much in the attacking midfield role that he had earned the nickname *'Platini'*. He possessed the perfect blend of power and skill, a willingness to work for his team-mates but also the ability to unlock a defence if the game wasn't going Boavista's way. Having struggled to make an impact at Benfica, Sánchez arrived in Oporto with a point to prove.

Having won two, drawn one and lost one of their opening four games, the next match against Benfica represented the first true test of where Boavista could aim their expectations for the season. With the big three having already dropped points, the match against Benfica would set the expectations for *As Panteras* going forward. An early goal from Brazilian striker Duda set the tone early, and from there on Boavista set about stifling the efforts of Benfica, ultimately coming away with a 1-0 victory. With two wins and two draws following, Boavista had collected 19 points from their first ten matches, but strong starts from Porto, Sporting, Salgueiros and Braga saw them in fifth place.

The first *O Derby da Invicta* was the perfect opportunity for Boavista to prove that their title push was serious this season. It took until the half-hour mark for the first moment of note, with a through ball from Whelliton finding Duda who managed to poke the ball into the path of the onrushing Martelinho, who put Boavista into a one-goal lead. With Deco being sent off just 15 minutes into the second half, and Boavista possessing the best defensive record in the league, the rest of the game was a mere formality.

A victory fully grounded in the characteristics of Pacheco's team, hard-working and solid at the back, the win was the highlight of a remarkable run. The 1-0 victory was representative of what Pacheco had aimed to build at Boavista and it was during the second half of the season that the defensive reputation that Pacheco's team had earned became apparent, with only six goals being conceded between the victory over Porto and the penultimate game of the season. The whole team worked towards this solid base, but it was the goalkeeper who was perhaps the ultimate player in keeping Boavista at the sharp end of the table.

A name familiar with an English audience, the man tasked with keeping the goals out was Ricardo, he of Euro 2004 fame. Ricardo was merely a rotational goalkeeping option for the *Chequereds*, often sharing the sticks with William Andem. The Cameroonian international had been number one heading into the season, starting the opening six games but, having conceded six goals in those games, the decision was made to bring Ricardo in, a decision that proved inspired. The goalkeeper would keep 16 clean sheets in his 28 matches, only conceding 16 goals.

With Porto having rediscovered their form, and a 1-1 draw away to Marítimo narrowing Boavista's lead to just four points, Pacheco's side could afford no mistakes. Key late goals from Elpidio Silva (1-0 against Farense) and Martelinho (1-0 against Sporting) kept the cushion at four points heading into the final few matches. An away trip to Salgueiros would be the setting for one of the most dominant performances of Boavista's season, with goals from central defender Litos, Duda and Silva firing them into a comfortable 3-0 lead at half-time. Two further goals from Silva completed the rout, meaning the team went into the last two games needing just a single victory, with their final match coming against their title rivals Porto.

For neutrals, a final game title showdown between two city rivals would have been perfect viewing. For Boavista fans used to living in the shadow of their more illustrious neighbours, anything but a victory over Aves would be disastrous. With Porto not playing until after, there were no distractions from the task at hand.

Just over 20 minutes had passed when Sánchez drilled a free kick low across the box, watching it get deflected into the net by Aves defender Soares. With the crucial first goal in the bag, Boavista kept pushing forward, led by Sánchez who seemed determined to drag his team over the finish line. As Silva bundled home his 11th of the season shortly after half-time, the atmosphere inside the Estádio do Bessa lifted. A third goal from Whelliton cemented the result further, securing the title from their arch-rivals Porto and finally dismantling the reign of the big three.

The entire club could be forgiven for not bothering with their last match, ultimately losing 4-0 to Porto. To the players, management and fans, that result did not matter. The only thing that counted was the final league table. Boavista had 77 points. Porto 76. For everyone involved at the club, the hope was that this was merely the beginning of a new age of Portuguese football, one where the big three would expand into a big four.

Title-winning teams are often defined by their best player, yet it was hard to truly find the superstar within the squad. Sánchez is the one name to stand out more than the rest, but the team was truly built as the sum being far greater than the parts. Everyone from Ricardo in goal to Duda and Silva up front worked for the team, with Roma coach Fabio Capello suggesting that there was 'no other team in Europe that runs as much'. Duda and Silva were the leaders of the Boavista attack, but neither managed to score more than 11 goals, an incredible feat for a team that managed 63 total league goals. This was the pinnacle for Boavista, the moment that their squad existed in a perfect balance of defensive and attacking quality.

With the domestic game conquered, Loureiro and Pacheco turned their attentions towards European success and sustainability. Courtesy of winning the league, the squad qualified for the following season's Champions League first group stage, earning ties against Liverpool, Borussia Dortmund and Dynamo Kiev. Having struggled a couple of seasons earlier to make a significant impact in the competition, there was a different atmosphere, a sense of belief emanating from their league triumph.

Two draws against Liverpool and home victories against the Germans and Ukrainians gave Boavista eight points after the group stage had concluded, tied with Dortmund for the second qualification spot. As Boavista had a slightly better goal difference, they progressed through to the second group phase where they would come up against Bayern Munich, Manchester United and Nantes.

Although their European run would end at this stage, they gave a strong account of themselves, picking up four points against Nantes and even holding Bayern to a goalless draw in Portugal. Having exited at the first group stage two years earlier, this run was a good illustration of the progress being made within the club. Sadly, with the increased exposure and appearances at the top table of European club football came increased demands for wages from players and staff. Their success on the pitch was becoming their downfall off it.

There was still time for one more run in Europe, however. Having finished second behind Porto the year after winning the title, they entered the Champions League during the qualifying rounds, defeating Maltese side Hibernians before falling to Auxerre, failing to reach the group stage. The Auxerre defeat saw the *Chequereds* slip into the UEFA Cup.

Rather than the convoluted group stage that haunts the Europa League presently, the UEFA Cup was simply a straight knockout competition. Drawn against Maccabi Tel Aviv in the first round, the tie started poorly, with the Israeli team winning their home match 1-0. An early own goal in the second leg settled any nerves, with Boavista eventually winning 4-1 on the night and 4-2 on aggregate. The second-round tie against Cypriot side Famagusta was an easier affair, with victory secured in both legs. The following rounds did not represent easier ties for the side, drawing them against Paris Saint-Germain, Hertha Berlin and Málaga. They managed to lose the first leg in all three ties, with crucial away goals in Paris and Berlin giving them a chance.

The second legs all followed the same pattern that had become the hallmark of Pacheco's team, a team that would battle until the very last whistle. Each game ended with a 1-0 Boavista victory, with the goal coming in the second half of each. Against PSG and Hertha Berlin, the victory was enough to secure an away-goals victory. Against Málaga, it sent the match to penalties, where Ricardo was once more the hero, scoring the first penalty and saving one to secure the 4-1 win in the shoot-out. For the fourth time in the tournament, Boavista had overcome a first-leg deficit to progress.

With both Porto and Boavista having reached the semi-final stage, everything was seemingly falling into place for a clash between the rivals to decide a major European final. Porto had comfortably dispatched Lazio 4-1 in their first leg, and Boavista had secured a 1-1 draw away to Celtic, giving them the slight edge. With just ten minutes remaining and the scores still level at 0-0, everything appeared set. What was unaccounted for was Henrik Larsson managing to fire home the winning goal, sending Celtic through and denying Pacheco and his squad the chance of winning a European trophy to mark their period of success.

And then came the true nail in the coffin. Rumours had begun to surface about the chairmen of the two Porto-based clubs using their influence to intimidate and bribe referees into calling decisions in their favour. Both Loureiros were ultimately charged, with João being given a four-year suspension by the Portuguese league, and Valentim being given a two-year suspension as well as a three-year suspended criminal sentencing. Boavista as a club were also impacted, being relegated down to the second tier. If being relegated due to a corruption scandal wasn't bad enough, a second consecutive relegation was to follow, sending the club to the amateur level of the Portuguese pyramid.

Having since been cleared of wrongdoing in the case, João Loureiro has set about making Boavista a solid top-flight team again, with the club being firmly placed in the top league since 2014/15. Yet this remains a long way from the glory days of the turn of the century. Loureiro and Pacheco took what can be considered a team of cast-offs and made them immortal. Through hard work, sheer persistence and the flair of Sánchez, Boavista dared to dream. For a brief period, Boavista became known for more than their unique shirts, managing to topple the big three of Portuguese football, a truly remarkable feat.

THE MAKING OF
JORGE JESUS

by Gareth Thomas *(@gareththomas54)*

IN THE first two decades of the 21st century, Portugal has been known to produce not just some of the game's best players, but also some of its most accomplished managers. The unprecedented success of José Mourinho with Porto in 2004 made Europe's top clubs take notice of the managerial talent to be found in the country.

A pattern emerged where domestic success would almost inevitably be followed by irresistible offers from abroad, with the likes of André Villas-Boas, Nuno Espírito Santo and Paulo Fonseca also making names for themselves overseas. Whether they be Portuguese coaches hoping to secure a move abroad, or foreign coaches hoping to add some silverware to their CV, managers at Portugal's 'big three' of Benfica, Porto and Sporting CP would rarely stick around for more than one or two seasons.

The country's most successful club, Benfica, had a particular habit of chopping and changing managers in the first decade of the century. After José Mourinho's brief two-and-a-half-month stint in charge in the autumn of the year 2000, no fewer than ten managers would occupy the Eagles' hot seat before 54-year-old Jorge Jesus accepted the job on 17 June 2009.

In some ways you could say that Jesus had come home. He was born in the Lisbon suburb of Amadora in 1954, the same year that Benfica inaugurated the original Estádio da Luz (literally Stadium of Light) just two miles away. By the time Jesus became the club's manager, what had been the largest stadium in Europe had been knocked down, replaced by the more modern stadium of the same name, in time for Portugal to host Euro 2004.

But despite the geographical links, no one could really claim that Benfica was Jesus's club. His playing career actually began with Benfica's arch-rivals, Sporting Club de Portugal, when he was spotted by a talent scout at the age of 15. He would never make the grade with the Lions however, as he became somewhat of a journeyman midfielder, appearing for 11 other clubs in total, mainly in Portugal's second and third divisions.

As a vocal player who never held back from barking instructions at his team-mates on the pitch, the signs were there that Jesus could have a future in coaching. And these qualities certainly stood out to Mário Rui, the president of lower-league side Amora FC, when his side came up against Jesus's team Almancilense. So impressed was Rui by the player's on-field leadership that he offered him a role as head coach at just 35 years of age.

Jesus accepted the offer, and by the end of the 1989/90 season he had led Amora to a third-place finish, a guaranteed promotion spot in Portugal's Serie F. And just two seasons later Amora were promoted again, this time to Portugal's second tier. Jesus couldn't keep them up though, and before the 1992/93 season was out, he had parted company with the club.

Throughout the 1990s and early 2000s, Jesus's managerial career would reflect his playing career, as he managed ten different teams on his journey from lowly Amora to Portugal's biggest club: SL Benfica. Spells at top-flight sides Belenenses and SC Braga made Jesus a viable candidate, though he was not the obvious choice for the coveted Benfica position, as they tended to prefer bringing in bigger names from abroad.

The country's biggest sports club were disappointed with their third-place finish in the Primeira Liga and the board came to an 'amicable agreement' with manager Quique Sánchez Flores to cut his two-year contract short a year early. Benfica had now gone four seasons without a league title and had failed to qualify for the Champions League.

High-profile managers from abroad had failed to bring success (Ronald Koeman had failed to retain the title won by predecessor Giovanni Trapattoni in his sole season in charge), while there was a reduced budget having failed to qualify for the continent's most lucrative competition for a second year in a row. As such, Benfica decided to try their luck with a more back-to-basics approach in hiring Jorge Jesus on a two-year deal, extendable by one year.

The Portuguese coach earned a lot less in wages than his predecessors and was not expected to last long in the job if his plain-talking style didn't get an immediate response from the underperforming squad. Luckily for the club's newly re-elected president, Luis Filipe Vieira, and sporting director, Rui Costa, the gamble paid off.

Right from his first press conference when presented as Benfica's new coach, Jesus made it clear that he understood what was expected of him in what was his biggest managerial role to date. When asked if he thought it would be a realistic objective to win the league in his first season, the Portuguese responded: 'Those who work at Benfica, whether as coaches or as players, can only feel satisfied if they are champions. There is no other objective.'

Benfica's new coach also took the opportunity to praise the quality of the squad at his disposal, and with good reason. The strong Latin American spine of the team was already in place. The Brazilian centre-back partnership of captain Luisão and a young David Luiz guaranteed a robust defence in front of which Argentinians Ángel Di María and Pablo Aimar could work their magic further upfield. That pre-season the club strengthened the side further with more South American signings. As Jesus opted for a 4-1-3-2 system, Javi García was brought in from Real Madrid to play as the holding midfielder behind a more attacking three of Di María, Aimar and fellow new signing Ramires, who would go on to play for Chelsea. Up front, Paraguayan forward Óscar Cardozo formed a 'little-and-large' partnership with former Barcelona prodigy Javier Saviola, who joined from Real Madrid in a €5m deal.

Jesus's side endured a shaky start to the season, but by the third match-week, everything had clicked into place, and in spectacular style. In front of a modest crowd of 40,000 on a warm Monday evening in Lisbon, Benfica hosted Vitória de Setúbal and sent the visitors home embarrassed, recording an 8-1 victory that sent a statement to Benfica's Primeira Liga rivals: this team was hungry for goals and hungry for its 32nd league title.

In the following weeks the goals kept flowing. The Eagles notched up 20 goals over their next five league games, as Jesus imposed his high-tempo style on the team. The Portuguese coach demands a lot from his players, but he always insists on communicating to them what they have to do, how to do it, and why they have to do it. In the Europa League the goal fest continued. David Moyes's Everton side were thrashed 5-0 at the Estádio da Luz in the group stage and Hertha Berlin were similarly dispatched in a 4-0 return-leg victory.

Then with a 3-2 aggregate win against Marseille, Jesus's side booked themselves a quarter-final tie against

Rafa Benitez's Liverpool. Yet despite coming from behind to win the first leg 2-1, the Portuguese side were powerless to prevent a heavy 4-1 defeat at Anfield. Jesus had brought an excitement and fearlessness to this talented side, but this would not be the year to end their trophy drought in continental competition stretching back to their 1962 European Cup triumph.

On the domestic front this Benfica side would have no such problems securing silverware. Despite a rare 2-1 defeat away to Porto in the penultimate round of fixtures, the Eagles clinched their first league title in five years, finishing five points clear of surprise runners-up Braga.

Jesus's two-striker system worked wonders for striker Óscar Cardozo in particular, who racked up 38 goals in all competitions in what was undoubtedly the best season of his career. The Paraguayan scored the final goal in Benfica's 4-1 League Cup semi-final victory against rivals Sporting in February and repeated the feat a month later, netting the third in Benfica's 3-0 triumph over Porto in the final.

Jesus would have to enter the next phase of his tenure with different players as he saw his star-studded side broken up that summer. Ramires and Di María departed for Chelsea and Real Madrid respectively. Marauding centre-back David Luiz joined his Brazilian team-mate in West London in January, and Benfica could only stand by and watch as André Villas-Boas's Porto side swept all before them domestically.

Over the next two seasons, it would be Benfica's European ventures that would grab the headlines. In a country where domestic titles come and go, the true barometer of success for Portugal's leading sides is to see how they fare against their European opponents. In this regard, Jorge Jesus did more than any other to restore the pride of a fanbase who keep alive the memory of the famous Benfica team of the early 1960s who, inspired by legendary forward Eusébio, won the European Cup in 1961 and retained it the following year.

After finishing as Primeira Liga runners-up, Benfica had to go through a qualifying and play-off round to gain entry to the 2011/12 season Champions League proper. They progressed to the group stage with comfortable wins over Trabzonspor and Twente, before being drawn in the same group as Sir Alex Ferguson's Manchester United, yet three draws (including two against Manchester United) and three victories were enough for Benfica to win their group. They then progressed 4-3 on aggregate against Zenit St Petersburg to set up a quarter-final tie with Chelsea.

The Lisbon side were unfortunate in the first leg at the Estadio da Luz, failing to score for the first time in 22 games as they fell to a 1-0 defeat despite having had the better of the chances. The second leg at Stamford Bridge was a feisty affair. Full-back Maxi Pereira was given his marching orders following a second yellow card in the first half, and Benfica were powerless to prevent a 2-1 defeat.

Nevertheless, Jorge Jesus could be proud of his side's efforts and they had proved that they could be a match for anyone on the big European nights. The next season Benfica were eliminated early in the group stage, giving them another chance to shine in the Europa League knockout rounds, where Jesus proved himself an expert at helping his team through two-legged ties, overcoming Bayer Leverkusen, Bordeaux, Newcastle United and Fenerbahçe en route to the 2013 final where they would take on Chelsea once more.

The London side were managed by Rafah Benítez, an old foe from the 2010 edition of the competition. In a close game Benfica had their fair share of the chances, but fate was not on their side. With the scores level at one apiece, Branislav Ivanovic headed home from a corner in the 93rd minute to hand victory to the Londoners.

It is said that Benfica are cursed by their European Cup winning manager Béla Guttmann, who, upon leaving the club in 1962, pronounced that the club would not be European champions again for another 100 years. The curse had proved to be spookily accurate in the years since, as Benfica lost the European Cup finals of 1963, 1965, 1968, 1988 and 1990. Now to the Benfica faithful it would seem that the curse applied to the newly created Europa League as well.

The 2013/14 campaign would be Jesus's fifth season, making him the first manager to hold on to the role for that long since Otto Gloria in 1959. It was also to be Jesus's most successful season in Portugal. Despite losing talisman Pablo Aimar on a free transfer that summer, and Serbian midfielder Nemanja Matić following the well-trodden path to Chelsea in the January transfer window, Benfica were dominant in the Primeira Liga. This was thanks mainly to the goals of Spanish forward Rodrigo and Brazilian Lima, who formed a strong partnership in Jesus's new-look line-up.

By 21 April they had sewn up the title with two games to spare. But there was plenty still to play for. With one piece of silverware in the bag, their next challenge was a Europa League semi-final tie with Juventus before competing in both the League Cup Final and the Portuguese Cup Final in May. After a 2-1 victory at the Estadio da Luz, Jesus's Benfica saw out a 0-0 draw in Turin on 1 May to return to the final, where they would take on Unai Emery's Sevilla, which coincidentally would also be played in Juventus's stadium in Turin.

First though, they had a Portuguese League Cup Final to play on 7 May, which they duly won 2-0 against Rio Ave to secure trophy number two. Next up was the trip to Turin and the chance to lay any talk of a hoodoo to rest. But the two sides remained deadlocked at 0-0 after extra time as the game went to penalties. Despite Lima netting Benfica's first, Cardozo and Rodrigo missed their penalties, handing the initiative to Sevilla, who duly dispatched all four of their penalties to take the trophy back to Spain. If there had been any sceptics of the Guttman curse before the game, there surely weren't many left now.

Despite claiming his side had been the better team, Jesus took the second successive final defeat on the chin, declaring in the post-match press conference: 'We have to leave this game with our heads held high. On Sunday there's yet another final for us. In football there's no point looking back.' And that message must have got through to his players, as on 18 May, at Portugal's national stadium, known popularly as '*Jamor*', Jesus's men completed a historic treble, sealing a 1-0 win over Rio Ave to lift the Portuguese Cup. This feat had never been achieved before in Portugal and although Benfica had won nine other doubles in their history, this was the first time they did so with a Portuguese manager at the helm.

Jesus went on to win another double the following season, capturing the league title and League Cup, in the process making him the most decorated manager in Benfica's history with ten titles. He was also the first Portuguese coach to win back-to-back league titles with the club. Yet Jesus's contract was up in the summer of 2015.

With all that he had achieved he had more bargaining power than ever, but Vieira, the president, didn't see his coach as irreplaceable. The cult of personality built around Jesus had made him not only too expensive, but perhaps also too popular and, on 4 June 2015, it was announced that negotiations on a new contract had broken down and Jesus's sixth season at the club had been his last.

The very next day Jorge Jesus was introduced to the media by his new club, none other than Benfica's arch-rivals Sporting Clube de Portugal. As thousands of fans welcomed him in the Alvalade stadium, a black-and-white video montage of Jesus's early playing days at Sporting appeared on the big screens. Jesus was visibly moved. His links to the club go back a long way, not least because his father, Virgolino António de Jesus, had also represented the club in the 1940s and registered his son as a Sporting member at 13 years of age.

Jesus took the microphone and announced to the crowd: 'From today onwards there aren't two candidates in Portugal. There are three candidates in Portugal!', raising three fingers in the air.

No one could fault the manager's ambition or self-belief, but ultimately, he wasn't the man to bring significant success to Sporting, winning just one Super Cup in 2015 and a League Cup in 2018. In the spring of 2018, the institution that is Sporting was thrown into turmoil, as thugs broke into the training ground and attacked the players just days before the Portuguese Cup Final, which they went on to lose to Aves in what would be Jesus's last game.

For some, Jesus's controversial move to Sporting could be seen as a betrayal. After all, he surely would have had offers from clubs all over the world. Yet the reality was rather nuanced. Back in 2015, Jesus regularly visited his elderly father who lived locally, and in his whole football career he had never played or coached abroad. With little knowledge of foreign languages and at 60 years of age, it is clear why a move just a few miles across town to his boyhood club was an attractive one.

As Portuguese coaches have earned a glowing reputation collecting trophies and spreading their ideas across the world, Jesus's successful career is testament to the fact that, for Portuguese clubs and managers, success can also sometimes be found by looking closer to home.

DRAGONS FOR THE FUTURE: A LOOK AT PORTO'S ACADEMY

by Danny Lewis *(@DannyLewis_95)*

AS IS the case in countries across the world, there always seems to be a battle for supremacy between the biggest clubs in Portugal. Porto, Benfica and Sporting Lisbon fans will often be looking at ways to get one over on their fellow domestic giants. There is, of course, bragging from whoever sits at the top of the league table, while references to historic achievements are made and arguments are had over who has the best academy in the country.

The breakthrough of youngsters is a source of pride for many, and that is no different for this trio – whether that is seeing someone shine for their own first team or being sold to a European powerhouse for big money. Benfica sold João Félix to Atlético Madrid in the summer of 2019, while Sporting's talisman Bruno

Fernandes left for Manchester United and immediately began making waves.

There will be constant debate about who has the best youth production line of the three clubs, but whether or not Porto's is the greatest, they can certainly claim that their academy has real significance on the shaping of their achievements. The influence this has for the club can be seen vividly through their biggest achievement in modern times – and one of their biggest claims to supremacy over the aforementioned rivals – their 2004 Champions League victory. This made them the first Portugal team to win Europe's flagship club competition since Benfica did so in 1962.

A team led by José Mourinho had comfortably progressed through a group that included Real Madrid, Marseille and Partizan Belgrade. That had then been followed up by wins over Manchester United, Lyon and Deportivo La Coruña. All of this led to a final against Monaco at Arena AufSchalke in Gelsenkirchen, Germany. As the goalscorers in that 3-0 victory, Brazilian striker Carlos Alberto, Deco, who was developed at Corinthians, and the Russian Dmitri Alenichev are likely the names that will be remembered in the history books. However, the base of that victory was largely homegrown, with three of their five-man defensive unit coming through their youth ranks.

Goalkeeper Vitor Baía, who made some vital interventions when the score was 0-0, captain Jorge Costa and his centre-back partner Ricardo Carvalho, had all developed at the club before going on to represent the first team. Porto can also lay claim to some credit for their nation's biggest success in recent times: their Euro 2016 victory. That is because João Mário, who played in the final, was developed at Porto before moving to Sporting Lisbon, while Bruno Alves, Vieirinha and André Gomes have all also spent time in the Porto youth ranks.

However, the academy has faced challenges and obstacles, with Porto having found a way of utilising obscure markets, mainly the South American one, to full effect. This is best highlighted by their Europa League Final victory against Braga in 2011. Only three Portuguese men – João Moutinho, Rolando and Silvestre Varela – made it on to the pitch in that game, though none of them were educated within the club.

It was a team that was heavily punctuated with South Americans, as three Colombians, three Brazilians, two Argentinians and one Uruguayan either started the game or came off the bench. It was also the iconic striker Radamel Falcao who scored the only goal of the game.

There is, perhaps, evidence that they are now striking up a balance where they are able to show astuteness in the transfer market, while also utilising their own talented youngsters to form a side that manager Sérgio Conceição can challenge domestically and in Europe with.

As is typical of any successful Porto side, there are those who were brought in from obscure sources: Otávio was signed from Brazilian outfit Internacional, Shoya Nakajima was recruited from Al Duhail and Jesús Corona signed from Twente. Though, alongside those and big stars such as Alex Telles and Moussa Marega, there are also signs that the club's academy are having an influence on the first team. Diogo Leite, Romário Baró, Vitor Ferreira and Diogo Costa are all youngsters who have been used sporadically in the 2019/20 season. Meanwhile, 27-year-old Sérgio Oliveira has also made an impact, having gone through the youth ranks and been on various loans to clubs such as PAOK and Nantes before coming into his own at home.

However, it is 17-year-old Fábio Silva who is arguably the most exciting of the lot – even arguably fighting for the crown of the most talented prospect currently plying their trade in Portugal. He joined the Dragons' academy as an eight-year-old with an inability to take the pain of defeat, though he did have enough ability on the ball to stand out ahead of his peers. The prodigal youngster did end up going to Benfica in 2015, as his brother, Jorge, was offered a move there. Though after the sibling moved to Lazio, discontent and Porto's efforts meant that he returned to the club where his heart was truly set after two years away.

Before he had even made a first-team appearance, Silva was already being compared to Cristiano Ronaldo by Sporting legend Manuel Fernandes, who told *SIC Noticias*: 'When Ronaldo was 17, he played as a centre-forward for Sporting's youth teams. I saw him doing things that I'm now seeing a boy from Porto do, Fábio Silva.'

Taking his own inspiration from Mauro Icardi and Edinson Cavani, Silva has made his way into the first-team set-up, becoming Porto's youngest-ever player at 17 years and 22 days old, when he came on as a substitute during the 2019/20 season's opening day. That has been followed up by the teenager taking the titles of Porto's youngest-ever player in Europe, as well as the youngest player to score for the Portuguese giants. His eye-catching performances and records have drawn the attention of European giants such as Juventus and Atlético Madrid. Though they won't be getting him on the cheap as, in November 2019, Porto signed him up to a contract that runs until 2025, which includes a hefty release clause of €125m.

While he is the biggest example of a Porto academy product standing out with their talent, there is much more evidence of them bringing through top-level youngsters. This comes with *Transfermarkt* suggesting that the club had four players in Portugal's most recent U21s squad, three in both the U20s and U19s, five in the U17s and two in the U16s. This highlights how consistently they have been able to develop talented players that can perform among the country's best in their respective age groups.

This current record is no accident or coincidence. In 2008, FC Porto Dragon Force was created by the club. On their website, they describe it as 'an innovative project that, under the motto "You have the power of the Dragon", breaks new ground in the sports training of boys and girls from 4 to 14 years.'

The school was made with the purpose of helping to identify young players who can go on to make an impact for the club, while helping them with other factors such as education. Since its inception, the project has grown exponentially: it begun expanding within Portugal in 2010, a school was opened in Bogota, Colombia in 2012, another was formed in Toronto, Canada in 2015, then the most recent international school was opened in Valencia, Spain in 2016.

While this growth is fairly impressive, it is results in terms of youth development that will be the true measure of how the project performs and it stands up well. One eye-catching statistic is that Dragon Force has helped to produce 25 per cent of the players in Porto's youth teams. That this is the case indicates just how influential the project can go on to be in their talent identification process. Considering the age range of those that participate, as well as the project's formation, it is natural that the results will begin to be felt in the upper echelons of the club's youth academy. It will also be intriguing to see how many players they are able to bring through from the school to the first team in the coming years.

Porto have shown just how far they have come regarding the talent within their academy in the 2018/19 season. They proved that they have the best Under

19s team in Europe, coming out on top in the UEFA Youth League. The Portuguese outfit topped their group, overcoming Lokomotiv Moscow, Galatasaray and Schalke. In their three knockout games, Porto beat Tottenham Hotspur, Midtjylland and Hoffenheim, impressively scoring eight goals in that trio of matches without reply to set up a final against Chelsea.

The Blues' first team may have only recently started seeing the benefits of the quality coming from their youth ranks, but Chelsea have been serial winners at youth level. In addition to the plethora of domestic titles they have won, the youngsters from London won the UEFA Youth League in both the 2014/15 and 2015/16 seasons, showing just how tough this opposition could prove to be.

The quality they possessed is also shown by how far some players have come in the short time since the final: Billy Gilmour has been given first-team opportunities, Conor Gallagher is on loan at Swansea City after excelling at Charlton Athletic, Mark Guehi is also with the Swans, while Tariq Lamptey has moved to Brighton & Hove Albion.

Porto had talents of their own though, as the aforementioned youngsters Costa, Leite, Baró and Silva – who have all represented the first team this season – played in the game. In addition to that, Diogo Queirós, who was their captain on the day, is currently out on loan at Belgian Jupiler Pro League side Royal Excel Mouscron. These talents were able to earn the

Portuguese outfit a 3-1 victory in the final. Fábio Vieira opened the scoring from close range in the 17th minute, before Daishawn Redan equalised for Chelsea in the 53rd minute with his head. Porto were not left downhearted by that though, as Queirós bundled the ball over the line to get the team back into the lead just two minutes later. Their last goal was the best of the game, as Afonso Sousa passed the ball to Baró, who backheeled it in return, for the substitute to volley into the net to secure the win with a quarter of an hour left.

What is interesting to see from that tournament is that Silva, the starlet who now has a release clause of €125m, was not actually the club's top scorer. That accolade fell to Baró, indicating that he is another youngster in the first team to look out for.

Aside from those who are now in the first team or out on loan, plenty of players who were part of that massive victory are now playing for Porto B. This is their under-23s team, who currently ply their trade in the LigaPro, which is the second division of Portuguese football. The rules for these teams' inclusion are that they must have ten players from the club's academy, with a maximum of three players over 23. This offers a real chance for youngsters to show their first-team managers that they can make the step up to playing senior football.

They are one of five B teams currently in the league, alongside Benfica, Braga, Sporting and Vitória de Guimarães. However, there is one thing that Porto's youngsters have done that none of the others have managed as of yet: winning the league. They didn't earn promotion due to the rules, but in the 2015/16 season they topped the table – having also previously been runners-up in the 2013/14 campaign.

To make their league win even more satisfying, they won by five points, while Sporting B came tenth out of 24 teams, and Benfica's youngsters finished just one point above the relegation zone. When looking at the earning of bragging rights over the other Portuguese giants, the UEFA Youth League and LigaPro victories have to be pretty big vantage points when looking at their academy's successes.

Across Europe, there are some clubs who have come to neglect their academies. This comes with the feeling that it is a better tactic to buy ready-made players from other clubs, rather than giving a chance to those coming through their own academy ranks.

However, Porto are going against this notion. They have shown that they can complete astute business in the transfer market in recent years, but their academy is still very much alive and thriving – if anything, they may have found a way to make it even more productive with Dragon Force. All of this could see them on the cusp of striking up the perfect balance of buying in quality and producing their own talent through the academy to achieve success.

ANDRÉ VILLAS-BOAS: THE FALL AND REVIVAL

By Edd Norval *(@EddNorval)*

ANDRÉ VILLAS-BOAS was the prototype of something new in football management: exotic, young and well dressed. There are many like him now, but his emergence as a managerial prodigy, tactically astute and innovative, helped provoke a rethink of the 'coach' role – no longer reserved to grey-haired men in their 50s – a notion particularly felt when he landed on British shores in 2011.

It wasn't only his nuanced understanding of football and relative youth that set him apart as a source of interest – a footballing buzzword just before social media really kicked in – there was another fact that galvanised armchair experts, *Football Manager* enthusiasts and amateur players alike. He'd never played football beyond youth level. His knowledge and interest in the sport were grounded in both practical and theory, particularly how the two intertwine around their continental philosophy, but without having ever really played it.

Villas-Boas carries with him a name in Portugal; descending from an aristocratic family, access has never been a problem – nor has means. Rather than softening his desire, instilling in him a sense of comfort, it seemed to provoke the young man into action, a trait that defined both his early route into football and, indeed, the trajectory of his career that followed.

The young coach's bookish approach and foppish appearance ushered in the new 'laptop coach' idea, as he was often spotted analysing opponents, when working under José Mourinho, battering away furiously on his keypad. It was this early strength – focusing on opposing teams – that provided his coaching foundation. Those able to analyse opponents' strengths and weaknesses in both a logical and systematic manner are bountiful in football. It's just like any occupation – with enough study, one can identify and, through experience, begin to decode what is happening in front of them, picking out different managerial flourishes, accents and styles.

What differentiated Villas-Boas from the rest of the pack, and still does to this day, is his empathy. Now termed 'emotional intelligence', a sought-after trait in football coaching, the young Villas-Boas would interpret the moods of training camps he was sent on assignment to report on. Having his own group of players to mould was the next step, yet it proved to be a considerable challenge.

It was the Portuguese manager's first job, but more troubling than his inexperience was his youth. However, lacking any real seniority over his players in terms of age, Villas-Boas consciously moulded his approach with this in mind. He enveloped himself in his player's lives, taking an interest in their families and conducting talks in the manner of a friend, not a boss. His youth and friendly approach didn't diminish his authority though, rather his scrupulous methodology and affable persona presented an aura of calmness and control – exactly what a side on the cusp of relegation required.

An instant success, he pulled the team from the bottom of the league to 11th place after the previous manager Rogério Gonçalves resigned in October 2009. The side's sharp turnaround and overachieving attacking football brought him back to Porto, his childhood side, this time as manager. Upon leaving his maiden club, he sent the players a text: 'I'm leaving you for a new adventure. I thank you for what we did together. Each one of you has made their mark on me at the start of my career and all in different and special ways.' It was a flourish that players still recall today.

At Porto, the momentum for the young manager, who would soon become international football's hottest young prospect, refused to abate. Having already cultivated an air of mystique, being Mourinho's 'eyes and ears', yet rarely in the spotlight himself, his success at Porto meant he'd no longer be a figure left in the background. Porto roared to victory after victory, with

Villas-Boas leading the side to the Primeira Liga's second undefeated season, picking up the Supercup, Portuguese Cup, Europa League and the league. Becoming the youngest-ever manager to lift European silverware, aged only 33, his single season at his former club thrust him into the spotlight. In June 2011, he resigned. The following day, once again following in his mentor's footsteps, Villas-Boas signed a contract with Chelsea.

Struggling to make an impact and clashing with senior players like Frank Lampard and Ashley Cole over tactical decisions, his choices being called into dispute in front of owner Roman Abramovich is how his tenure is best remembered. Poor results early on meant that pressure mounted from every angle and with the side falling from the top four, Villas-Boas's contract was terminated shy of nine months in, his reputation hinging on a swift recovery, lest he be viewed as a flash-in-the-pan success. Many believed he'd succeed with time, but the Abramovich era was unprecedented in its demands for instant glory.

A chance at redemption came from fellow London side Tottenham Hotspur, who had recently unceremoniously parted ways with Harry Redknapp despite his success with the club. Alongside the personal pressure of reputation, Villas-Boas had big boots to fill. His personality, completely at odds with Redknapp's sharp wit and animated character, found a home at Spurs, the perennial challengers to the country's top four. Breaking their dominance, as Redknapp had come so close to doing the previous two seasons, would be viewed as a success. Anything less than a tight challenge, a failure.

Picking up two Premier League Manager of the Month awards (December and February), Villas-Boas led Spurs to their highest-ever points tally. The Portuguese *treinador* will be particularly fondly remembered by one man though: Gareth Bale. In large part, due to the manager's interpersonal skills, he was able to embed himself in his player's psyche and resolved to grant Bale the positional freedom he felt would help him flourish. It did.

Finishing the season on 72 points, a club record, it also held a more unfortunate one – the highest-ever for a side to accumulate without making it to the top four. Finishing one point behind Arsenal and without the allure of Champions League football, Villas-Boas lost Bale to a lucrative world-record transfer fee of €100m to Real Madrid. Clearly acknowledging Bale's impact on the side, Villas-Boas made an effort to sign figures capable of filling the void, but also to help shape the side in his image.

His choices for replacement, from Erik Lamela to Christian Eriksen and Roberto Soldado were long-term *kind-of* fixes – not the identical replacement sufficient to mount an increasing challenge the following season. Despite spending a considerable amount of money on new players over the summer, Villas-Boas was gone by

December 2013 with the highest win percentage of any Spurs manager to date.

Graceful and devastating attacking plays defined Villas-Boas's tenure in Tottenham, but poor defensive organisation overshadowed his glowing efforts, ultimately costing them their pathway into Europe's big league. Partly redeemed, a new challenge was in order, both culturally for the naturally nomadic coach, as well as in a place lesser known – a move to provide him time out of the spotlight to really begin refining his tools, something that his early success negated the need to ever do. Villas-Boas, as of March the following year, was bound for Russia's second city, the eclectic and colourful Saint Petersburg.

Zenit are one of post-Soviet Russia's success stories. Since the dissolution of the Soviet Union in 1992, Russian football lacked a truly reflective federation and league, which it gained in 2001 with the foundation of the Russian Premier League. Four months after waving London goodbye, Villas-Boas was in charge of Zenit who, having won the league in 2010 and again in the 2012 season, were struggling under Luciano Spalletti and hoping for a phoenix-like turnaround from the early textbook of Villas-Boas's Portugal years.

Football in Russia then was best known for two things: Andrey Arshavin and their violent ultras. Classy or elegant are two fairly rare adjectives. A dead end to many, it was an open door for Villas-Boas, a fertile plot of land from which to carefully cultivate a blooming crop. Again, the invigorating effect Villas-Boas seemed to have on his previous sides emerged from the get-go here too, with Zenit winning their first six games under his tutelage, the first coach to do so in the newly founded league.

Usually dominated by the Moscow sides, Zenit pressed hard, ending his debut campaign one single point behind champions CSKA with the silver lining of a Champions League place. Building on his first album success, Villas-Boas didn't allow the pressure – thankfully a lot less pervasive than in England – to interrupt his process and, despite being knocked out of the Champions League group stage in a sticky pot with Monaco, Bayer Leverkusen and Benfica, Zenit would go on to win the league that year.

Another reasonably successful season – on paper – followed, with a final-16 place and Russian Cup trophy, yet Villas-Boas had more pressing issues. Media were accusing him of boring 'anti-football', underachieving for a side of their capacity. His uncharacteristic caution hinted at a deep aversion to further hindering his career progress. So, on a high, coupled with his want to explore, the manager decided to return home for some family time.

Many adventurous types struggle in hiding their ambition and want for seeing the world. Villas-Boas is no different. Heeding the siren call of quiet familial life prised him away from Russia's cold grip, but life in his homeland wasn't enough to keep him for any amount of time. Barely six months after leaving Russia, he was on a plane to China.

A friendly figure in football, understated and driven, it would be a mistake to think of Villas-Boas as a pushover. On occasion, his temper has previously flared. Iberian passion fizzes through his veins in these moments, a trait in old wives' tales attributed to his fiery hair colouring. In China, Villas-Boas the wide-eyed young man of management was decidedly more mature, clearly growing into his skin. Yet his time in China will be remembered more for his antics than achievements.

It's not to paint his experience in Asia in a bad light, simply that his puritanical views of football and sportsmanship were sullied by something Villas-Boas seemed to feel were institutional – namely corruption and cheating in the league. He arrived at a side that weren't viewed as true contenders – Shanghai SIPG were an outfit seemingly destined to test the top spots in the Chinese Super League, yet never fill them. Taking Sven-Göran Eriksson's seat as club manager, Villas-Boas was unable to bring home any titles yet built a side who seemed set on shedding their image. Finishing a respectable third behind Fabio Capello's Jiangsu Suning and perpetual champions Guangzhou Evergrande Taobao, he had created something truly worth being proud of. Unfortunately, it seemed to go almost unnoticed.

In a country where order rules, and those going against it are punished decisively and harshly, Villas-

Boas's cool European demeanour was tested. Firstly, after one of his players started a mass brawl by kicking the ball at his opponent, the Portuguese coach got a two-match ban for his reaction on social media praising Oscar's previously clean disciplinary record, taking a subtle jibe at the severity of the eight-game ban.

Now with his own record for suspended games beaten, Villas-Boas's solo ban would supersede his previous one in length – by six games. After one of his players was denied a penalty, he furiously ran up to the official with members of his coaching staff, resulting in an eight-game ban for abusing the official and 'aiming an offensive gesture at him' that was still being seen through upon his exit. Alongside repeated accusations of officials favouring Guangzhou Evergrande, Villas-Boas felt stifled and decided to leave and make up for lost time, embarking on a sabbatical to pursue another dream of his – the Dakar Rally.

Entering the 2018 edition as a co-pilot, the vehicle he was competing in collided with a sand dune, a fate far more severe than it may sound. Exiting the competition with a severe back injury and reluctant to return to management until he could do so with the gusto he desired, it truly was time for a break. Villas-Boas had been a sensation, but quickly fell victim to the expectations his early success incurred. Then, in 2019, he made his comeback.

Rudi Garcia left behind a Marseille side – to join rivals Lyon, no less – that finished the Ligue 1 campaign

30 points behind winners Paris Saint-Germain in fifth. With a side full of promising talent, the recently established new ownership had to make a pivotal choice in replacing him. Marseille can, and should, be present at the high end of European football, yet a tumultuous history pocked by *did-that-really-just-happen* moments has always kept glory just out of reach.

Villas-Boas and Marseille both have had a lot said about them. They've hardly been quiet agents in the game. Not that Villas-Boas desired attention, but the world's interested eyes have always followed his globetrotting exploits. Yet, in each other's embrace, they've found a sort of kindred spirit, like two young punks coming of age, settling down into a new phase of their lives. Marseille needed someone who fitted the 'mould' – that inexplicable thing so many iconic clubs have. The Portuguese man and the French side aren't that different. Both have shown potential, both fallen short and both are hoping for a steady redemption.

That Villas-Boas specialises in the development of players, nurturing them to both express and perform at their highest levels, is paramount to the side that boasts such exciting young talent as Duje Ćaleta-Car, Lucas Perrin and Boubacar Kamara who are, interestingly given his previous defensive records, all defensively minded players who have bolstered the foundations of his firebrand side.

Not to mention the mentors in the side either. Long-serving Florian Thauvin and the unexpected success story and talismanic presence of Dimitri Payet are the glue who, before the world break in football due to the 2020 COVID-19 pandemic, were sitting strongly in second place, just behind Paris Saint-Germain. The waves he's managed to make in France have gone by in the media like ripples. Villas-Boas's reluctance to give interviews or spend time in the spotlight has meant that his club's huge success – one which could arguably be Europe's biggest turnaround – has gone by almost unnoticed. Under these circumstances, with less pressure than ever before, the conditions are primed for him to excel.

The only catch is his burying of the ghosts of Russia. Villas-Boas is playing a conservative brand of football in France, albeit one that is succeeding. Stability, at most clubs, is highly sought after. But Marseille, the *enfant terrible* of European football, may have limited patience for such an approach, unless trophies start returning to the Stade Vélodrome. Under Marcelo Bielsa's short stint there, fans were treated to a scintillating thrill-ride; his pitchside presence continually roused fans – not that it takes much for the South of France side.

Even under Rudi Garcia, Marseille made it to the Europa League Final, meaning that while expectations aren't sky-high as they were for Villas-Boas's time in the Premier League – they still exist. Creating his own managerial path was never going to be easy for Villas-Boas – living in the passenger's seat of a personality as large as Mourinho is bound to cast a shadow. Moving away from this, into a character of his own, has defined his career, arguably, more than the football itself.

In his earliest mentor, Bobby Robson, through the Englishman's love of attacking football, Villas-Boas found his greatest influence, more so than Mourinho – the two only really showing similarities through their relationship, nationality and initial paths, rather than style of play. Having spent a lifetime as a student of the game, achieving his goal of using football as a means of seeing the world, understanding various cultures and methodologies, his personal debt to Robson, as well as individual philosophy developed over time, has culminated in his recent success at Marseille. Villas-Boas probably has his last real shot at the big time in Marseille and, if his early time there is anything to go by, we could see a new era of André emerge.

PORTUGAL, EURO 2016 AND A WINNING MENTALITY

By Kaustubh Pandey *(@Kaus_Pandey17)*

'MENTALITY MONSTERS' has become a phrase vaguely thrown around. Be it due to popular social media coinage or the abilities of concerned teams alike, the term encapsulates the fighting mentality in sides that fans adore. But before social media permeated people's lives as much as it does today, many 'mentality monsters' would often not get as much credit.

While examples are numerous and can be found around every corner of the football world, putting context to other cases gives us more examples. The Portuguese national team is one of those that will go down in history as the winners of Euro 2016. But history might not bat an eyelid at the context, background and how Fernando Santos's men rose from the ashes. In this step-by-step process, they came a long way in a 12-year period.

What made the final of Euro 2004 even more painful was the effort that went into it and that the heartbreak came at home. At the Estádio da Luz in Lisbon, Luiz Felipe Scolari's men had registered 17 shots on goal, while Otto Rehhagel's Greece side had just five. In what was a pragmatic performance by the Greek outfit, Portugal were kept out of the game in fascinating circumstances. The nullification of Cristiano Ronaldo, Deco and Luís Figo had rendered the team useless at that point. Reaching the final was a high point for the country in itself. But the World Cup of 2006 proved to be a similar heartbreak for Scolari's side. Having beaten England in the quarter-final of the competition, they went on to lose to France in the semi-final. The sort of progress the team was making led to nothing once again and Euro 2008 showed that.

Despite these disappointments, there was always hope that perhaps there was something special coming their way. The country has always had players who had the flair to change games. Be it Figo or Deco in 2004 or those like Nani and Ricardo Quaresma in 2016, there was no shortage of players with flair. They had defensive players who oozed grit and tigrish spirit. The evolution of Cristiano Ronaldo in more aspects than one bound the team close from 2012 onwards.

Strangely enough, Fernando Santos was in charge of Greece in Euro 2012. Paulo Bento's Portugal wasn't short of any talent at all – like it was for the editions before 2012. They were far from being the favourites to win the tournament though, as the team seemed incomplete in some regards. While Ronaldo was at his everlasting peak, there was hardly any other world-class talent bar Fábio Coentrão, João Moutinho or Pepe.

The tournament had seen Ronaldo score half the goals, indicating a reliance on the then Real Madrid man. There wasn't a concrete system which could bind them together – something that did lift Santos's side of 2016. But if there's anything Euro 2012 did for Portugal it was that it gave many players in that team vital experience of competing at that level. They acquired the know-how of going far in international tournaments, with Ronaldo inducing them with immense fighting spirit and steel. Pepe and Bruno Alves were regulars under Bento, marshalling the backline on a consistent basis. José Fonte had acquired a reputation in the Premier League, while Ricardo Carvalho had come back to the fold.

Moutinho and Quaresma grew in stature, while newer talent in Danilo, André Gomes, William Carvalho and João Mário came up the ranks and were attracting attention from bigger clubs. Renato Sanches was seen as the budding superstar, while Raphaël Guerriero was growing through the ranks at Lorient. Like Fonte, Southampton had given Cédric Soares the platform to play for the national team on a regular basis. This was the coming together of not just Portuguese players playing club football in the country, it was a mixture of varying talents playing in different countries.

Luckily enough, a lot of these players would have grown up watching the loss to Greece back in 2004. It is anyone's guess if that chip on their shoulder had a part to play in what unfolded. There was the burden of making the nation proud after decades of disappointment in the knockout stages. The challenges of potentially stiffer teams in Italy, France and Germany lay in front of them. Belgium were growing as a force while England had been the perennial dark horses.

The qualifiers to the tournament had seen Santos use a 4-3-3 shape. It hadn't started off too well, as they took a shock 1-0 loss to Albania in the first qualifying game in 2014. But the team stuck together for the rest of the games, letting in only four goals in what was left of the campaign. They were never a free-scoring side as a lot of those wins came by a one-goal margin. But the identity-creation process was underway, and Santos knew what he was doing.

Ronaldo had scored only five times in qualifying, as the approach to the game was far from pragmatic. *Os Navegadores* would concede cheap goals, something Santos had growing concerns about with the tournament approaching – that, despite the team having a raft of experience at the back in Pepe, Bruno Alves and Fonte and sitting midfielders like William and Danilo Pereira.

Many selections at the Euros were rather expected. Sanches, who had sealed a big-money move to Bayern Munich, deserved a call-up. André Gomes was shining at Valencia and he earned one too. The impressive and consistent Adrien Silva, upstart in Rafa Silva and hard-working Wolfsburg full-back Vieirinha earned their spots in the side as well. But one of those selections raised many eyebrows.

Eder's 2016 started on the bench for Swansea City away to League Two Oxford in the FA Cup. It wasn't unexpected to witness two of the Swans' best prospects – Daniel James and Stephen Kingsley – remain on the bench at the Kassam Stadium on that night. Strangely enough, Eder was occupying a spot beside them and didn't play a single minute despite the side's 3-2 loss.

His arrival from Braga in the summer of 2015 had been an utter failure. He hadn't scored a single goal and hadn't registered a single shot on target. Despite having cost €6.7m, he made just two starts and was consistently relegated to the bench behind regular striker Bafétimbi Gomis. Soon after that appearance on the bench against Oxford, Eder was loaned out to Lille as he went in search of regular football and more goals.

His spell at Lille wasn't a bad one by any means. But for a striker who wasn't too prolific back at Braga, it was a strange selection. Eder was to play back-up to Ronaldo, and many thought he hadn't done enough to warrant a spot like that. He was certainly the odd one out.

What came as perhaps a bigger surprise was Santos's formation change. Pitted alongside Iceland, Austria and Hungary in a tricky group, his insistence on using the 4-4-2 took many by surprise considering it was different in the lead-up to the tournament. This shape had Ronaldo play regularly as the striker beside a deep-lying forward in either Quaresma or Nani.

From the very beginning of the tournament, further doubts crept in for why Santos had brought the tactical change. Portugal didn't win a single group-stage game, leaking a cheap goal against the surprise package Iceland. They let in three goals against a fellow pragmatist in Hungary but held out for a 3-3 draw. The performances weren't pretty by any means whatsoever. Santos had resorted to playing a brand of football that was pleasing very few.

There were murmurs about how the side was playing a 'dirty' style of football despite having players who would relish the chance to play attacking football. But all that mattered was the team's progress into the knockout stages. Another slip-up in these stages could've brought back familiar memories from the years gone by. But the group stages had been concrete proof that while they wouldn't win convincingly, they wouldn't lose either.

The round of 16 handed them a stiff tie against Ante Čačić's Croatia side, one that had a similar sort of vibe as Portugal in terms of how they were viewed in the tournament. They had Mário Mandžukić playing up front, with Milan Badelj and Luka Modrić in the double pivot. Around him, Mandžukić had Ivan Rakitić, Marcelo Brozović and Ivan Perišić. But Portugal had a plan to combat the talent against them.

Santos nullified them. Perišić hit the woodwork once and, while Croatia had 17 attempts on goal, none of them were on target. Quaresma won the game for Portugal, scoring in extra time and making an impact from the bench. It was a performance that had defined the team's playing style. The traditional 4-4-2 had midfielders in Gomes and João Mário often playing as wide players. They would drop in central areas off the ball, allowing the opposition full-backs to come forward and allow Ronaldo and the second striker constant two-on-two situations.

Poland were the opponents in the quarter-finals. Portugal were favourites to win the game, but doubts had been creeping into people's minds. The *Seleção* hadn't won a single game in normal time and, to many, it was a case of riding on pure luck and fortune. For Santos, it was far from it as 4-4-2 it was against the Robert Lewandowski-led Poles.

When the Bayern Munich star found the net in the third minute of the game, the fears of many were coming true. But with their backs to the wall, Portugal showed a slightly different side of themselves. Sanches, the emerging star in the team, levelled up before the first half ended and Santos urged his team to get a goal before the 90 minutes ended. That didn't happen, as another Portugal game motored into extra time and then penalties.

And the jackpot – as people were making it out to be – worked to Santos's benefit. A Jakub Błaszczykowski missed penalty handed the Iberian side a spot in the semi-finals. Pepe and Fonte enjoyed impressive games as Poland were wiped out in familiar circumstances. More than this being fortune, it was now beginning to look like a game plan. This had become the team's identity: dig games out, manage them and take the chances whenever they come.

The semi-final against Wales was the team's best chance of coming closer to redemption. And the clash against Gareth Bale's side was the only game Portugal won in normal time. Goals from Nani and Ronaldo saw them through comfortably, as France beat Germany to make it to the final. There were no guesses for who the favourite was going to be. Didier Deschamps's men knew that it was easier said than done.

One reason why Santos's side became synonymous with Ronaldo was because of how they embodied each other. The team was a lot like a collective version of Ronaldo himself. It was far from as technical as the older generations. But through the Real Madrid man and the manager, they had the tenacity and will to win at all costs even in the direst situations. In a tournament that would go down in history as one for the pragmatists, Portugal were perhaps meant to win it. They were to win it one way or another – like Santos and Ronaldo would like.

The Stade de France was packed to capacity. Portugal had been in this situation before. But stylistically, they were now at the opposite end of the spectrum. They were happy to concede possession to France and rely on the counter-attack – like Greece were 12 years ago in Lisbon. But the hushed silence that fell over Stade de France in the 25th minute would gather global headlines. Ronaldo had to be taken off due to injury and, in him, Portugal had lost not just the invincible leader, but they'd lost the aim for long balls from the back. Mentally and tactically, this was a blow.

But it became a blow that France couldn't take advantage of. Ronaldo the player was incapable of playing. But Ronaldo the motivator was having none of it. Like his mentor Sir Alex Ferguson would, Ronaldo was clutching to the sidelines and urging his team-mates like they might never get another chance to win this. And the players obeyed. They fought for every ball in their bid to cancel out a collectively better unit in *Les Bleus*. They had two managers to look up to.

There was a point when everyone was resigned to watching a Portugal game go into extra time. Strangely enough, Santos rolled his dice and took Renato off for Eder. The then 28-year-old hadn't scored even once in the tournament as they now went 4-3-3 with Eder up front. Chances were few and far between as France were pressing and constantly on the front foot.

What came in extra time is the sort of unlikely miracle that Eduardo Galeano would go about the world for. The most nondescript of players in Eder himself wrapped his foot around a Moutinho pass in the 109th minute of the game. The shot evaded everyone, including Tottenham goalkeeper Hugo Lloris, to kiss the back of the net. No one – not even Eder himself – could've ever imagined anything like this happening when he was the unused sub on that dreary night at Oxford in January.

It was the untying of several knots – like a thriller novel or a motivational sports movie. There was an unlikely hero who came out of nowhere to rescue his country. There was that superstar who nearly had his dream broken in a final but led his team to the win without even playing. There was disbelief, as many had believed that this team wouldn't go on for too long. It was the completion of a full circle and the burying of the ghosts of the past.

The fact that this victory came in a similar manner to that of Greece was another speculator subplot. It was meant to be so, in a tournament that was glittered with pragmatists and the undervalued. This was a footballing fairy tale that might not go down as one of 'mentality monsters'. But to the romantics, it would be the unlikely story of another underdog uprooting the big boys in 2016.